Ten Traps of Television

Ten Traps of Television

by Francie Taylor

Post Office Box 1099 • Murfreesboro, Tennessee 37133

Copyright 2003 by
Sword of the Lord Publishers
ISBN 0-87398-895-7

Printed and Bound in the United States of America

Contents

Introduction vii
The Remote Control Test xi
1. The Time Waster
   (Psalm 90:12) 1
2. Dulling Your Light
   (Matthew 5:16) 11
3. Hindering Your Prayer Life
   (Psalm 66:18) 17
4. Discontentment for Sale
   (I Timothy 6:6–8) 23
5. Sowing Seeds of Spiritual Confusion
   (Isaiah 5:20) 31
6. Developmental Problems in Young Children
   (Proverbs 29:15) 39
7. Cultivating Rebellion and Worldliness
   (Proverbs 24:1, 2) 61
8. Spoiling Christians in Their Later Years
   (Proverbs 16:31) 75
9. Marriage Pollution
   (Colossians 3:18, 19) 81
10. Glorifying 'Strange Womanhood'
    (Proverbs 5:3–5) 91
11. A Plea to the Leader of the Home
    (Psalm 119:37) 101

Introduction

Television is the the modern-day "drug" of choice. How addicted are you to its mesmerizing power? Is your TV on in the background right now as you read this book? If so, you are like a large number of Americans; but as a Christian, you would be counted as a soldier who is entangled in the "affairs of this life" (II Tim. 2:4). An entangled warrior is a limited, hampered fighter in any battle. Your television choices could be leading you to give up some valuable territory in your heart and mind. Is *entertainment* worth such a price?

We live in a culture that loves to be entertained at almost any cost. The word *entertainment* is derived from the French word *entretenir*, which means "to hold between." Many people are being *held captive* by the various forms of entertainment currently available. The trouble with this captivity is that there is growing evidence of a direct relationship between the decline in common decency and the consumption of today's popular entertainment. We are entertaining ourselves to death!

Even if this obsession were a problem for just the

unsaved world, we would still have a massive job on our hands as we navigated our way through an increasingly impolite, hardened, rage-filled society raised on perversion in a box. Unfortunately, Christians are also being massively affected by watching programs, renting videos or viewing things on the Internet at which they would never glance twice if Jesus were seated beside them in the room.

If you are a Christian, Jesus is in the room when you watch TV; and unless you are impeccable in your viewing choices, He is probably not very pleased.

God never meant for us to adopt the customs and ethics of this 'wicked and perverse generation.' Romans 12:9 tells us that we are to "abhor that which is evil" and "cleave to that which is good." Television lures us to imitate and eventually become that which is not acceptable to God. If you don't believe this, listen to the young people talking the next time you're around a group at church. The English language as it is used today reflects the incredible disorderliness of our current generation. After years of viewer indoctrination, Christians are sounding, looking and acting worldlier than at any other time in history!

You do have a choice. You can either continue to pretend that there is nothing wrong with watching TV programs that influence you to be a carnal, worldly Christian, or you can face the truth about the insidious infiltration of television programming and determine to do something about it.

Introduction

It's time we stopped allowing the enemy to have the keys to the front doors of our homes via the television. As an appliance a TV is harmless, but once you turn it on, you are at great risk of needing the "Pollution Control Agency" to come in and decontaminate your living room!

It is a well-known fact that television programs are not the only bad influences on our society, but television remains one of our most readily available forms of corruption. From toddlers to the elderly, just about anyone can gain access to a TV. You don't even have to own one anymore. Just stroll through a mall, go to an exercise gym, or even sit in the waiting room at the doctor's office. Public places abound with free TV!

We have many forms of media today that have the potential to influence our thinking adversely. The Internet is rife with dangers, causing even the secular world to cry out for more protective devices against the smut sites and spam mail from perverts. Video rentals allow people to provide movies to the family that may not be intended for all ages. Video game units are becoming common in homes with young people, while video games, which used to be good, clean fun, have mutated into cartoon replicas of pornography, prompting the industry to provide us with ratings for games!

Yes, there are multiple opportunities to roll in the mud these days, but television remains the simplest form of "decline by design."

Introduction

If we are ever going to be "wise unto that which is good, and simple concerning evil" (Rom. 16:19), then we have to examine carefully where we stand in relation to our use of media forms such as television. This takes a conscious effort on the part of the viewer.

The choice is clear and simple: *control the remote*, or you will end up *living under remote control!*

The Remote Control Test

Is television so important that you can't imagine life without it? Take this test to see if you are in charge of the remote or under remote control.

You may be under remote control if

1. you have watched a show that had foul language and didn't turn it off or change the channel;
2. you have watched a show that had nudity (partial or full) or inappropriate sexual situations and didn't turn it off or change the channel;
3. you have watched commercials that were offensive or sensually suggestive but didn't turn them off or change the channel;
4. you watch talk shows that are not news related;
5. the TV is on for background noise;
6. you have turned on the TV to entertain (baby-sit) the children or sent them to go watch TV so that you could get something done;
7. you have allowed your children to watch shows that have disrespectful, violent or otherwise inappropriate

characters (cartoon or human);
8. you are afraid to set TV standards because you think that your children would revolt;
9. you schedule your life around certain TV shows;
10. you watch TV in bed to fall asleep;
11. you ask people to call you back because you're watching TV;
12. you know several television characters by name;
13. you own a giant-screen TV;
14. you can tell everyone what's wrong with TV but you keep watching!

Well, how did you do on this test? If more than five of these items are true in your home, you may be under remote control. Only you know your own home, but if it is your goal to 'set no wicked thing before your eyes,' then it is time to reconsider your current TV viewing habits in order to limit or reduce this infectious influence in your life.

"I will set no wicked thing before mine eyes: I hate the work of them that turn aside; it shall not cleave to me."—Ps. 101:3.

Trap One
The Time Waster

"So teach us to number our days, that we may apply our hearts unto wisdom."—Ps. 90:12.

Time—don't you wish they sold it like phone cards? We could go up to the cashier and say, "I'd like five hundred extra minutes, please." She'd take our money and give us more time. We could wish for such a dream to come true, but in reality, time is a vaporous entity from God that we cannot buy, replace or invent. Knowing how precious a commodity it is, why would we want to waste time?

Think like a runner for a moment. If you wanted to cause your opponents to lose the race, slowing them down would give you an advantage—right? Distracting them so that they would waste even a few seconds could give you the opportunity needed to defeat them.

We have an enemy who thinks like that! "Let me get them to watch just a few minutes of TV," he plots. A few minutes (and a few hours) later, we're still in the same place, channel surfing in search of something that will make us feel better about wasting our time. Time wasted is time lost, and time spent watching television is time that is no longer available to us for more important activities.

Less Time for Bible Study, Prayer, Family Altar

With the dramatic increase in spiritual immaturity and apathy today, it's evident that many Christians are not spending regular time in Bible study. Just ask any preacher who has ever played the trick on his church family, "Turn in your Bibles to the Book of Hezekiah," and he'll tell you how much page rustling he heard from the pulpit! Contrary to common opinion, daily Bible reading is not optional for Christians who are serious about their lives in Christ!

If people spent even one-tenth as much time per day reading their Bibles as many do watching the latest folly on TV, families and churches would be in much better shape. According to the A. C. Nielsen Company (1998), the average American watches 3 hours and 46 minutes of TV each day (more than 52 days of nonstop TV-watching per year). By age 65 the average American will have spent nearly 9 years glued to the tube.

Ten percent of 3 hours and 46 minutes would be roughly 23 minutes. While 23 minutes is less than the average TV sitcom, it would amount to a great investment in the spiritual development of a growing Christian if it were spent reading Scripture instead of watching television. Twenty-three minutes of Bible reading certainly beats none!

How much time have you spent in Bible study today? Now compare it to how much time you've spent watching TV or using other electronic distractions such as video games or surfing the Internet. If you're an average Christian, you are probably in the hole spiritually. Instead of hiding God's Word in your heart that you might not sin against Him, you are storing up a toxic treasure trove of images that have the power to sway you to live what you see.

If Bible study suffers, the prayer life will follow. We won't be spending time in sweet fellowship with the Lord, because television dulls that God-given desire, causing us to draw away as we build up iniquity in our hearts through illicit viewing habits.

The effect of television on our young people is already a concern, but it is compounded when it disrupts family worship time. And when Dad and Mom aren't interested in their Bibles personally, they aren't going to be in a hurry to conduct a family altar. In fact, with the TV on in the same room, who would even want to think about the things of God?

Face it: the less time you spend in the Word, in prayer or having family altar, the less you will care about how you use or abuse the gift of time. The enemy wins by distraction!

Less Time to Run an Orderly Home

"Be it ever so humble, there's no place like home." The new, revised version would probably go something like this: "Be it ever so *harried,* there's no place like home!" Many homes today suffer from neglect, both in upkeep and overall management. Television, the great time-robber, keeps us from taking care of our homes like we should.

Since the "keepers at home" job was given by God to the woman (Titus 2:5), it is often the woman who is being *kept* from doing her job by the lure of daytime programs. Mothers have an even harder time in this area if they are at home full-time during the day, because it is very tempting to use the TV as a built-in baby-sitter for young children or as "adult company" while folding laundry or doing other tasks.

Once again, the enemy misses few opportunities to slow us down in our spiritual race, so it's no accident that some of the worst programs for a woman's heart and mind are on TV during the day!

Soap operas, also known as "dope operas," have long been the vehicle of advertisers touting their latest wares to the unwary housewife. Although we don't call ourselves "housewives" anymore, we're still a favorite target market to advertisers. In fact, women are doubly distracted and poisoned while watching the soaps, as the commercials are sandwiched between program segments that contaminate the mind with perverted relationships, an unbalanced emphasis on worldly examples of romance and a general lifestyle of unreality.

We "keepers" need to be busy doing our jobs. If we were employed by a company and spent their time watching TV instead of doing what we were hired to do, we'd be fired and pronto! The problem is our perspective. We don't see our "jobs" at home as designated positions from God; therefore, we place little value on doing those jobs "as unto the Lord."

Laundry, housecleaning, dishes, dinner and other tasks are all done with more attention if the TV is turned off. If you've grown accustomed to having the TV on all day, try a day without it and see if you don't get at least twice as much done, if not more. Make a list of things you've been putting off until you "have more time," then get going on those house projects with the television firmly in the "off" position.

Down Time for Dad?

Men who work away from the home all day have little if any opportunity to watch TV. The problem for many men comes when they walk through the door, tired and anxious for a break from a hard day's work. It is common for men to unwind in front of the evening news or other programs.

Today's average news program has become little more than transportation for the latest propaganda, as well as a highly sensationalized marketing competition. It is important to know what is going on in our world today, but it is becoming increasingly more difficult to get the news without all the fluff and filler.

The Time Waster

When men with families watch TV beyond the news hour, they risk inviting the enemy into their homes to attack both them and their vulnerable loved ones. The shows available for viewing after the evening news are designed to snare the viewer into watching thirty- to sixty-minute segments of mind-numbing carnality at best, mind-warping filth at worst!

There is simply no justification for watching a sports show that has scantily clad cheerleaders bouncing around on the field or court. A person doesn't need sports to sustain life, but purity of heart and mind *are* essential to sustaining the spiritual well-being of a Christian.

When a man compromises in his TV viewing habits, he not only dulls his senses to spiritual things, but he runs the great risk of breeding a spirit of resentment in his wife or children as they take a backseat to the television.

Reality-based police shows, wrestling programs and other "guy shows" are also great thieves of time, as well as affection robbers. Closing yourself off from the family to park in front of the television sends a loud and clear signal to your family that you prefer the people on TV to the people in your home. You will never have the time again that you have right now in the lives of your family members. Do you really want to choose TV characters over them?

Less Time for Ministry

People are truly busy today, but not as busy as they pretend to be. Many simply choose to use their spare time to watch TV. Sadly, this practice has spilled over into important areas such as our ministry time. Pews are half empty because many people would rather stay home and watch TV than go to church, especially on Sunday and Wednesday nights.

Visitation and soul-winning programs compete with popular

prime-time shows. Special meetings and missions conferences compete with TV miniseries. Sunday night services compete with Sunday night sports events. Ministries on any weeknight compete with cable TV with its hundreds of channels worth of viewing choices. No wonder people think they're so busy!

We are at a time in history where soul winning, visitation, revival meetings, missions conferences, Bible studies and just basic church attendance are desperately needed. People are also needed to run or assist in these ministries. If you're "busy" watching TV, or even just relaxing in front of the TV instead of going to church, you are shortchanging yourself spiritually.

People aren't becoming more lukewarm these days by accident. If you are a regular TV watcher, spiritual things are bound to seem dull to you by comparison. Whether your mind is being exposed to trash or trivia, your heart is growing cold, or at least indifferent, to the things of the Lord. You are still running the race, but the enemy has now erected high hurdles with your permission, and you are not able to clear them.

Take an honest look at how you have been using God's time lately. Are you really too busy to help with a ministry such as Vacation Bible Time, or is it that you'd really rather sit and soak in front of the tube? Are you really so pressed for time that you can't attend Wednesday night service, or have you chosen to have a carnal service with your television "friends" instead? Are you chronically late because you don't have enough time, or have you lost track of time while dwelling in the imaginary world of television?

It is eerie to drive through a residential neighborhood at night and see how many homes have now upgraded to large-screen TVs. You can't miss them as they emit a large, blue glow through the windows that is visible from half a block or more away. In fact, you'll see that familiar blue glow in some cases very late into the night hours.

The Time Waster

"I'm too busy." We all have duties, but as Dr. Bob Jones, Sr., used to say, "Duties never conflict." In many cases, conflicts arise because people have wasted time. We wouldn't have nearly as many time constraints if we'd simply be willing to reduce the amount of time consumed watching TV.

Ministries today need committed Christians who are willing and able to say "yes" when asked to help out. If you think that your church can run everything on just the church staff alone, then you are woefully deluded! It takes an entire church family, or at least a large portion of it, to make a ministry run effectively.

What have you done lately to help with the needs of your ministry? And which TV shows are keeping you from doing more?

Less Time for Others

Have you ever phoned someone and had her ask you to call back because she was watching something on TV? Do you know people who make their plans around a favorite show? Are you perhaps one of these people?

Why spend time talking with real people when you can invite a houseful of artificial guests? We are living in the age of unreality, and modern guests and companions have become electronic ones. Spending time with TV "friends" is the latest way to fellowship!

We miss many opportunities both to give and receive blessings when we fail to make time for others. Whether it's visiting elderly parents and helping out around their homes or hosting missionaries on furlough, people still need each other. Television not only takes up the time that could be invested in others, but it also crowds out the desire to be helpful. Instead of considering what could be done for others, a TV-saturated heart asks, "What's in it for me?"

Developing a heart for others requires the work of the Holy Spirit, both through our reading of the Word and from hearing the preaching. Since lukewarm Christians have very low motivation to read Scripture, they tend to rely heavily on the preacher to feed them their weekly ration of the Word. These are also the types of people who are very slow to volunteer to do anything that would interfere with "their time," which includes but is not limited to their TV time.

If television is allowed to become a regular "resident" in your home, you will eventually find that it graduates from resident to master, crowding out the real people in favor of the ones who live in the electronic box!

A Floating Sense of "Not Enough Time"

You've probably heard variations of this lament before: "I just don't have enough time." Actually, we have all been given the same amount of time, but we choose to use it in very different ways! Some believe, as Scripture teaches, that we are to "number our days," which makes us desire to live wisely. Others foolishly abuse the hours, which eventually add up, creating a self-inflicted time deficit.

There are many people today who are plagued by a feeling of being on an endless treadmill called life, with no time off for good behavior. In actuality, the time off has been squandered, and once it's gone, it's gone! If you've been feeling like you never have enough time, ask yourself this question and do an honest, hour-by-hour evaluation: What do I do with my time?

Our days are numbered, whether or not we learn to live like it. The question we must ask ourselves is this: Will I throw away my time watching inane foolishness and depravity on TV, or will I dedicate my time to the Lord and let Him lead me on how best to use it?

The Time Waster

If God reigns within your heart, you will not struggle with His instructions to 'number your days'; but if the television is your master, don't be surprised if it always seems like you're running out of time.

Think about it: "I will set no wicked thing before mine eyes," said the psalmist (Psa. 101:3). "Pass the television programming guide," says the modern man.

Trap Two
Dulling Your Light

"Let your light so shine before men, that they may see your good works, and glorify your Father which is in heaven."—Matt. 5:16.

I will never forget the scene I witnessed in the dry cleaner's years ago. I was standing in line (sort of a captive audience) waiting to drop off some items while a woman in front of me was waiting to pick up her items. A man was with her.

The cashier brought out what appeared to be a formal dress. It was under plastic, so the woman removed the plastic bag to examine the garment. That's when the action really heated up!

"My dress!" the woman yelled, pointing to a large spot that looked like it had been splashed with bleach. "Look what you've done to my dress! You'll pay for this! It's totally ruined!" She went on and on like this for a couple of minutes, while the man with her tried in vain to calm her down. One thing that was noticeable about the whole scene was that the cashier hadn't said one word so far, which was an unusual display of self-control considering the verbal tirade he was enduring.

When the cashier finally got his turn to comment, he made this statement: "I can't believe we go to the same church!"

Pause for a moment to imagine the impact that this statement had on the raging woman. Picture a jaw dropping to the chest as the woman's face turned crimson. All breathing was momentarily suspended in this room.

Have you ever witnessed the facial changes of a person as he melted down from a combination of shock and embarrassment at the same time? It's not a pretty sight.

The line I was standing in had grown, and we all let out our own individual gasps before we could catch ourselves. The lady who was previously ranting went from red to pale and became amazingly speechless. Her companion dropped his head and looked at the floor.

Who needs TV when people act like that in public today?

This woman sounded just like the shrill, modern-day, "I'll-give-you-a-piece-of-my-mind" type that exists in the land of television. The big difference is that TV people have no real consequences, while we here on Planet Earth do pay real prices for our transgressions.

Can you imagine how this woman felt when she realized that she was chewing on the hide of someone (previously unknown to her) from her very own church family!

This scene was not funny. It was sad but representative of the manners of our day. It's tough to be a light in all this darkness, but it's even tougher if our own selfish, carnal living obscures our light.

Could that have been you? Are you so well trained by the smart-aleck TV role models of our day to overreact to life's irritations that you'd let loose with your tongue if you felt like it?

Reflections of a TV Diet

Whether or not researchers and media pundits want to admit it, there is a direct relationship between the increased crudeness of our society and the downward spiral in television decency. We are victims of an increasingly selfish, bad-tempered and

Dulling Your Light

out-of-control culture that is nurtured by TV. Dark and angry countenances reign supreme, while tongues that utter vicious or corrupt words abound. In fact, you can tell what's popular in both appearance and behavior without even watching TV, because the culture so readily reflects a steady diet of their favorite shows. The problem is, a dark countenance coupled with a foul, out-of-control tongue have no place in the life of a Christian who desires to shine as a light.

"Be not deceived; God is not mocked: for whatsoever a man soweth, that shall he also reap" (Gal. 6:7). You not only *are* what you watch, but over time you *become worse* than what you watch!

"Imitation is the sincerest form of flattery," or so the saying goes, and many Christians today are either unwittingly or willfully imitating the culture around them, particularly by watching, then impersonating the speech and mannerisms from the characters on the "hot" TV shows.

Look at the faces as you walk the halls of your church. How many are radiating the light of the Lord? How many are smiling, not only with the mouth but also from the eyes and from the heart?

What do you look like on a daily basis? Is your countenance dark and surly or bright and pleasant? Your facial expression, which is a large part of your countenance, will either radiate a diet of the Word or a junk-food habit of TV and other heathen forms of media. Just as our bodies malfunction when we routinely feed them poor fuel, our hearts and minds suffer damage from wrong food as well!

We can't overcome the costly effects of a bad TV habit by simply putting on nice clothes and wrapping ourselves up in a package of token church attendance. Our countenance will still tell on us, and others will be repelled by our lack of godliness.

Ten Traps of Television

Who Can Tell What You Are?

Television programs do a great job of blurring lines that are meant to be quite sharp and defined. We can claim to know Christ as Saviour, but when we expose ourselves regularly to TV, the world will have a very difficult time distinguishing us from them. This is because we become programmed to look and act just like them! The lady in the dry cleaner's is a great example of what happens when we forget that we are ambassadors for Christ.

How do you react to life's daily situations? Do minor annoyances send you over the edge? Maybe you've never made the connection between your television viewing habits and your personal behavior, but there is one.

Today's popular television programs portray and validate inappropriate behavior every day. Even if you're not watching the three-hour-per-day average, you are still sowing seeds of bad ideas in the data bank of your mind.

Are you imitating the world in its behavior, language style or manner of dress? Are you trying to keep up with what's currently fashionable according to the world? Are your personal standards based on what's popular or on what's scriptural? Have you ever stopped to ask yourself exactly where you are getting your ideas and standards?

If you are trying to be both *in* the world and *of* the world, you will run the risk of becoming a worldly, fence-riding Christian who lives a life of pain and frustration. Worldliness robs us of our ability to be salt and light, because worldliness naturally focuses the attention on fitting in rather than on pleasing God. Television programs feed the "conform-and-be-like-us" mentality just like a restaurant buffet feeds the masses.

People Repellent

When shopping in a large department store awhile ago, I

Dulling Your Light

noticed a sterling silver bracelet in the showcase. It stood out because it was badly tarnished. The price tag was visible, and the price was fairly high, but the bracelet looked used and neglected. In other words, I wasn't drawn to it; I was repelled by it. If that store wanted me to buy that piece of jewelry, somebody needed to clean it up and make it shine again!

When we call ourselves Christians but fail to shine as lights, we are like that piece of jewelry: of great value but cloaked in a repulsive veil of tarnish. Worldly Christians don't draw people to Christ—they repel them! The worldly, carnal lifestyle sends a confounding message and becomes a stumbling block to the unbeliever.

Are you a good advertisement for Christ, or are you a walking "people repellent"?

Are you trying to be a witness at work while at the same time you know everything about the latest TV shows in full detail? How are you going to get around to talking about Christ when you're laughing with your unsaved co-workers about the foibles of your television "friends"? You won't draw them to Christ with your double-standard way of life, but you may hinder them from ever coming to Christ with your ineffectual testimony!

Life is not a talk show, and we are in a battle—not on a game show. We need to be very alert as soldiers and servants of Christ, and we simply can't be alert if we've become entangled in "the affairs of this life" (II Tim. 2:4) by saturating our hearts and minds with the derangement found on TV.

Matthew 6:23 sums it up clearly: "But if thine eye be evil, thy whole body shall be full of darkness. If therefore the light that is in thee be darkness, how great is that darkness!"

Think about it: When asked if she thought that a person

who doesn't watch TV would be qualified to write about the dangers of today's television programs, pastor's wife Mrs. Valerie Clear replied, "Yes! You *want* to go to a doctor who is NOT sick."

Trap Three
Hindering Your Prayer Life

"If I regard iniquity in my heart, the Lord will not hear me."—Ps. 66:18.

Every time you watch something on TV, an image enters your mind. What your heart does with that image is another step in the process. If we were talking about a computer, we would call it programming. The mind is a God-given "computer," capable of the same type of input-output functions that we have in our electronic versions.

What kinds of images have you been entering into the data bank of your mind lately? Violence? Simulated crime? Pornographic scenes of "lovers" engaged in a wide variety of immoral behaviors? No matter what the vice, TV can dish it up at the click of a remote.

When we watch things that God didn't mean for our eyes to behold, our highly imaginative minds shift readily over into a fantasy life, retaining the images for future reference. If our eye gates are left unguarded, they become like a breach in a walled city, allowing rubbish to enter into our hearts and minds, causing us to 'regard iniquity in our hearts.' God is clear about this: If we regard iniquity in our hearts, we might as well go out in the backyard and pray to the squirrels. God will not hear us!

TV Trivializes Sin

Where do you think so many Christians got the idea that sin is not so bad? If the enemy had to go from house to house one at a time and try to convince us that we can sin and it's okay, he'd never get to all of us. But if the enemy could have a vehicle that would pass this message to countless millions at the same time, his task would then suddenly become remarkably easy, and he would achieve a great victory!

Television is not real life! I repeat: *Television is not real life!* Watching too much television can convince you otherwise, but your thinking that unreality is real, doesn't make it real. Sin is real, and unanswered prayer is real, and trouble is real, but television programs are the unreal products of a writer's mind.

Television programs have long been employed by the "prince of the power of the air" to tempt and distract us and distort reality. While the Lord would have us pure in heart and mind, the enemy would love to see us stuck in the same old mud from our old unsaved lives, regardless of whether we're rolling in that mud or just imagining that we are. Remember, since the enemy can't have our souls, he'll settle for destroying what's left of our lives!

Trivializing sin causes us either to attempt to continue to live in sin or to nod to and wink at those who do. We learn to rationalize sinful lifestyles by feeding on the television images of corruption and moral impurity. The more we regard the iniquity, the duller our senses become, causing us to tell ourselves that we're okay when we're really in foul condition!

What do you think of divorce? Do you hate it, or have you come to accept it as just another option when a marriage doesn't work out? How about your stand against fornication or adultery? Is it wishy-washy because you have overexposed your mind to the lifestyles of the rich and famous with their date-of-the-week-club mentality? Have you grown accustomed to the sight of people passionately clutching each other on TV, or does it still jolt you enough to get you to change the channel abruptly?

Has television slowly conditioned you to accept scantily clad women as normal, so much so that it doesn't offend or even faze you when you see a woman jogging in nothing more than a bra and biker shorts? Perhaps you have become convinced that you need to show more skin in order to compete with the modern-day harlots being molded by popular TV. Perhaps you routinely dress in the "less-is-more" custom of today—when you're not at church, of course.

Once we learn to regard iniquity in our hearts, we become a friend of the enemy. After forging this dangerous liaison, it's a very short time until we're justifying sinful behavior in our own lives. Even if you would never actually engage in the misbehaviors routinely witnessed on your favorite shows, you will still hinder your prayer life and stunt your spiritual growth by allowing your mind to dwell upon such sin.

Television isn't the only vehicle capable of causing us to fall, but it is the most common, and its capability to ruin is greatly underestimated.

Unanswered Prayer

My son was calling throughout the house for me one day, and he finally came down to the laundry room where he found me engrossed in sorting laundry while both washer and dryer worked in the background. "Mom, I was calling and calling you," he said. I didn't hear him when he was calling me, so he didn't get an answer.

If God will not hear your prayers, your prayers will go unanswered.

Ten Traps of Television

We have an epidemic today of people making unwise choices and claiming to have prayed about it. God is not and will never be the author of confusion, but you could easily come up with a host of conflicting and confusing "answers" if you are feeding on the swill of TV and then presuming to go to God in prayer.

Do you want answers to prayer? Of course you do. Are you willing to quit bowing to your golden TV calf in order to reduce your exposure to the customs and habits of the world? Are you willing to confess to God that you have sinned in your viewing habits? Are you seriously repentant or just sorry that it has cost you?

"But I've prayed to God, and He just hasn't answered me," so many people lament.

Is there any possibility that you have been regarding iniquity in your heart in front of your television set and then you dared to go before a holy God to make requests while dripping with your wickedness?

First John 1:9 reminds us, "If we confess our sins, he is faithful and just to forgive us our sins, and to cleanse us from all unrighteousness."

Your confession is as sincere as the repentance that accompanies it. If you mean business when you confess your sin, then you must turn away from that sin by the power of the Holy Spirit. How utterly foolish to assume that we can repeatedly disobey God on purpose and then go to Him demanding answers to prayer like a petulant child demands a treat!

Selfishness is a definite way of regarding iniquity in our hearts, and television promotes selfishness as a religion in and of itself. When we think so highly of ourselves that we imagine we can live in constant, presumptuous sin and remain in fellowship with God, we are deluded at best, demented at worst. Regarding iniquity in our hearts is hazardous to our spiritual, emotional and possibly even physical health!

Poor Deposit, Poor Return

When I was in elementary school, one of the local banks had a savings program designed to teach young children how to deposit and save money. Every week we would put five or ten cents into a red and white envelope and give it to the teacher, who would then put all of our individual envelopes into a larger one and give it to the school office. The school office would then take our deposits to the bank.

Periodically, we would each be given a little passbook that would show us how much money we had in the bank and how much interest it was earning. As you can imagine, our little accounts didn't grow very fast, as they were too tiny to earn much in the way of interest. Even so, by the end of six years in elementary school, everyone who had participated in the program had a decent savings account. To this day, I still remember the lessons of deposit and return.

Television programs deposit pictures in our minds that remain there. The purpose for this retention (also known as memory) is so that the mind can make "withdrawals" from the "data bank" at a future time. God is very interested in what we deposit into our "mind banks." The Devil is also interested in our deposits and is willing to give us some help in making the "image bank" grow larger, faster and fouler.

Just as you earn a small amount of interest on a small bank account, you get a poor return when you deposit poor-quality materials in your mind. We get only one mind, and we can either fill it to the brim with corrupt information, or we can make deposits that will reward us properly for years to come.

It is very difficult to regard iniquity in a heart that is filled with Scripture. Notice that I said it is very difficult, but it is not impossible. You see, we are all capable of actively, willfully choosing to sin.

One of the key differences between the victorious Christian life and the defeated one is the diet of the mind. Psalm 119:11 clearly explains this principle: "Thy word have I hid in mine heart, that I might not sin against thee." The Christian who feeds his or her mind improperly will have more trouble with temptation than the Christian who nurtures the mind with the high-quality, steady diet of the Word of God.

It makes no sense to add to the struggles of daily life. We will all have trials, tribulations, occasional heartaches and many other unexpected twists and turns. Why would we want to add the burdens of an unclean mind coupled with a life of unanswered prayer? There is no legitimate reason for such a choice.

Are you regarding iniquity in your heart by watching things on television that you wouldn't even glance at if the Saviour were seated beside you in the room? Well, you need to remember that He's even closer than that, if you are saved. He's in your heart, and He knows and sees all that you do.

What have you been watching lately, and how's your prayer life?

Think about it: We have never had more opportunity to think and meditate on impure things than today. To guard the heart, we must shield the eyes!

Trap Four
Discontentment for Sale

"But godliness with contentment is great gain. For we brought nothing into this world, and it is certain we can carry nothing out. And having food and raiment let us be therewith content."— I Tim. 6:6–8.

Have you ever wondered how much less money you would spend if you didn't have a television? Our family has had firsthand experience with an unintended experiment in this area.

When my husband gave me permission to eliminate network television from the lives of our children several years ago, I had no idea how much it would affect their seemingly insatiable appetites for toys, games, junk foods and other items. By the time they had been out of the after-school-TV habit for a year, they no longer even knew nor cared what was "hot" and what was not in the toy world. Now that they are teens, we have an even greater blessing of not being exposed to the latest fashions portrayed so regularly on television.

Quite by accident (or, more accurately, by God's design), we had removed an enormous *shopping stimulant* from both their lives and ours. Christmas these days includes just about any gift, handmade or purchased. We've even had several years of shopping at the local dollar stores for gifts, with no complaints from a single recipient!

When TV or other shopping stimuli do not infect you, clothing doesn't have to have a brand name or somebody's first name splashed across the front or back. When you don't really know what's "in," you are free to shop for what you really like without the added pressure of trying to conform to the latest fad or trend. Clothing just becomes clothing, and toys are picked based simply on their ability to provide some fun!

While the TV-addicted child may want another electronic video game unit, the limited-TV child would have as much fun with an indoor game as he would going outside with a bug net to chase dragonflies. The TV-addicted child has very little fun when a TV isn't included, while the child with limited TV time still finds pleasure in ordinary playtime.

When your life isn't deluged with advertising, your shopping scales down to purchasing needed items, with wants and frills brought under control. We know what we need, when we need it and how much we can afford to spend. Advertisers present us with more information than we need, in order to cultivate buying impulses that would otherwise not exist. It's what they call creating a market.

The serpent in the Book of Genesis used a similar tactic to that used by advertisers on us today—attack through the eyes. "And when the woman saw that the tree was good for food, and that it was pleasant to the eyes, and a tree to be desired to make one wise, she took of the fruit thereof, and did eat, and gave also unto her husband with her; and he did eat" (Gen. 3:6).

Advertisers want you to desire what you see, so they make their wares very "pleasant to the eyes." After they have your eyes, the advertisers have a very short walk to your mind and your money.

Mind Control at Its Finest

Television served no real purpose until advertisers took it

Discontentment for Sale

over. You would have had a very hard time convincing hard-working Americans of the post-Depression era to sit around watching pictures flashing across a screen in a box if they could be out working instead. Prior to the TV age, free time was spent reading, working with the hands on some sort of craft or sitting around the family radio.

Once people earned their money the hard way, they were not quick to part with it. The mentality of the average family of the 1940s was to save money, not spend it. Changing the minds of such a group was going to require a strong tool. That tool was television, and now it's more powerful than ever.

Advertisers target people today by markets or groups. The male group has a different type of advertising aimed at it than the women's group, while there is still another type used for children. Senior citizens are also targeted with specific types of ads.

If you are a man, how many cars or trucks have you owned since you've been driving? How about your father or your adult brother? Men are the favorite target markets of vehicle manufacturers. There is something about the sight of a shiny new car or truck that sends a man's hand straight to his "Hip National Bank" for the checkbook! Add a beautiful woman or two, some fancy maneuvering around curvy terrain, zero-percent financing and of course some music (usually rock), and they've hooked their big fish!

While visiting my grandma a couple of years ago, I saw a car commercial on her small living room TV that caught my attention. This particular car company chose a popular rock song in which the singer repeatedly said he wanted to get away. The message that I got from that commercial was that a man could simply buy that particular car, speed around a few tight corners, and he would then be getting away from life's realities.

Ten Traps of Television

This is fantasy at its finest. In real life, happy husbands want to get away from work and go home to their families. In the TV life, men want to get away from it all, especially their families.

While men are being courted by the car industry, women are targeted by the "looks" industry. We are constantly blasted with ads for anti-aging creams, hair colorings, diet pills and potions and, as we start to age, menopausal magical tonics. We are never pretty enough, never have the right color hair, always need more "powder and paint to make a woman what she ain't," and above all, no matter what we weigh, it's way too much!

No wonder there is an epidemic of depression in our society. With women constantly being told that they don't measure up, and with their spouses also exposed to false standards for feminine beauty, it's a real wonder women aren't collapsing from the weight of the pressure itself!

Children, the advertisers' latest wonder-market, are easily overexposed to things that they don't need, given the incredible average number of hours that American children spend watching TV. Advertisers hawk their toy wares all year round to our little ones. The heaviest toy advertising is still before Christmas, but since the pump is primed and ready, it doesn't take much to get little Junior begging for the toy of the season months ahead of December.

Toys are often paired with unhealthy foods and are aimed at our children like a double-barreled shotgun. Children today are facing diseases, lacking in exercise and struggling with excessive body weight in previously unheard of proportions.

Who's whetting their appetites? Whoever it is that can afford a loud, colorful ad between their cartoon bites. Usually, the pizza, cereal and burger companies have the most money and therefore the greater ability to create false hunger in an unwary child.

Discontentment for Sale

With movie companies tying their licensed toys to fast-food restaurant chains, children are given yet one more reason to want to go out to eat. To young eyes, these powerful, carefully marketed and diligently planned commercials are irresistible. Several sentences of nagging later, a parent is at the drive-through window with a happy child in the back seat.

Senior citizens aren't exempt from target marketing either. Many seniors today take several medications at a time, while experiencing little or no improvement in their overall health. While it would be irresponsible to imply that drugs are entirely unnecessary, it would likewise be foolish to assume that the multitude of drug advertisements have no effect at all on those who might be experiencing health problems in their later years.

Senior citizens, who often spend long hours in front of a TV and use it for companionship, are being taken advantage of in a cruel way. Ads combine the creation of false need with fear to convince the senior consumer to head over to the doctor and ask for the latest prescription. Other items, such as expensive home security systems and health-aid gadgets, are being peddled as if they were vital to life.

No one gets left out of the advertiser's gunsights!

Never-Enough Syndrome

Are you grateful for the home in which you are currently living, or are you looking for a new "starter castle" with more power to impress? Do you buy or lease new cars often because you want to have a newer model, even if your older model runs fine? Do your closets overflow with items that were purchased because they were a good deal, but now you have no real use for them?

If you answered "yes" to any of the above questions, you may be suffering from Never-Enough Syndrome.

Regular exposure to advertisements can cause a person to

develop a severe case of Never-Enough, otherwise known as *ungratefulness*. It has already been established that advertising exists to get us to lust after wants, not needs. Armed with this information, consumers would be extremely prudent to examine their current purchasing habits in order to resist the additional stimulus provided by TV ads.

Advertisers are telling us what to wear, what to eat, where to live, what to drive, and even what drugs to take. The more a person is exposed to television and its wares, the less able he becomes simply to make his own buying decisions. The advertisers do our deciding for us!

God never meant for Christians to be snared in this way. When we truly take a hard look at our checkbook registers or credit card statements, we are able to see clearly how much or how little we are influenced by materialism and consumerism. With television, advertisements are cleverly sandwiched between shows that depict people who are living consequence-free, spendy lifestyles without any evident cost. TV characters don't have real debt problems, but *real* people have real debt problems!

The More You Spend, the More You'll Work

Hollywood actors often live in opulent homes, both on television and in real life. Their displays of materialism are peddled to us via the magazine racks at the grocery store, as well as on shows about the rich and famous. No one ever seems to ask the obvious, like, "How much time do you actually spend living in your mansion, Mr. or Ms. Hollywood?" What good does it do to have a sprawling expanse for a home if you rarely get to do more than sleep there?

People have bought into the show-me-the-money mentality of today. "Image counts," the world says. Whose image? What kind of image?

A great evangelist who was preaching at our church years

Discontentment for Sale

ago said something like this: "People spend a lot of money on things that they can't afford, trying to impress people that they don't even like." That about sums up the picture.

Since image is so significant these days, advertisers have taken advantage of this perceived importance by creating a tidal wave of nonessentials. People are wired for sound today, talking or even arguing on their cell phones in just about any public place (including church)! Cars come outfitted with more optional equipment than ever. (I do not personally care to know the exterior air temperature on a winter day in Minnesota. I just get in the car and crank up the heat!) Appliances resemble computer systems and are obsolete just about as fast.

Everywhere you go, people are displaying their material badges of honor. All the while, advertisers are busy cooking up their next "gotta-have-it" offerings.

Are you spending money to attain a lifestyle that has nothing to do with what God wants for your life but has much to do with your exposure to advertisements and artificial lifestyles?

When you have to work longer hours to maintain an unnecessarily high standard of living, you don't own your things: *your things own you.* It's like signing up for a bizarre form of slavery in which the slave not only works for his master, but he pays the master too! The master, your possessions, will push you and prod you until you drop from the exhaustion of trying to maintain a plastic image of feigned wealth.

An additional sad side effect to attempting to promote an image of personal wealth is that it will greatly limit your circle of fellowship. Bible commentator Matthew Henry said this: "Prosperity makes people proud and forgetful of God, as if they had no need of Him."

Having too much can actually cause you to think too highly

Ten Traps of Television

of yourself, thus leading to fellowship with only those who are from your circle of affluence. In Proverbs 30:8, the writer wisely asks, "Give me neither poverty nor riches," as the ground is safer in the middle, while there is potential danger at the extremes.

We don't lack *things* in America; we lack *contentment*. Advertisers are seeking to perpetuate this, and they will continue to breed discontentment for as long as they exist, because if we're satisfied, we're not buying unnecessary things. In fact, studies are done on a regular basis to find out how to make and keep us discontented so we will be shoppers and buyers for life.

Look again at God's "math formula" from I Timothy 6:6: Godliness + contentment = great gain.

On the other hand, worldliness plus materialism equals great bondage and loss.

It is important to know what follows in the next verses: "For we brought nothing into this world, and it is certain we can carry nothing out. And having food and raiment let us be therewith content" (vss. 7, 8).

People will never remember the list of possessions you have acquired in life, but they will likely remember who you were and what you did. You can choose godliness with contentment and experience God's riches, or you can copy the rest of the world as they throw themselves off the cliff of financial instability in a fruitless search for fulfillment through things.

Which lifestyle do you really want?

Think about it: A machine washes our clothes while another dries them. Our ovens cook the dinner while we're away from home, and our dishwashers scrub the pots. Our cars map the routes and monitor our fuel levels, but...the next television commercial is going to try to make us feel deprived.

Trap Five
Sowing Seeds of Spiritual Confusion

"Woe unto them that call evil good, and good evil; that put darkness for light, and light for darkness; that put bitter for sweet, and sweet for bitter!"—Isa. 5:20.

We don't need television to teach us how to be wicked. We come equipped with that knowledge in our own sin nature. Television is more like the fertilizer on the sinful soul-weeds of our lives. Once we fertilize these weeds, which were growing fine but less quickly on their own, the gardens of our hearts become overrun with giant, life-choking weeds of sinful habits and patterns that are very hard to root out.

People today don't have a tough time seeing themselves as good people because they are comparing themselves to those whom they deem to be more wicked than themselves. The Apostle Paul had to address this type of mind-set in II Corinthians 10:12: "For we dare not make ourselves of the number, or compare ourselves with some that commend themselves: but they measuring themselves by themselves, and comparing themselves among themselves, are not wise."

Comparing ourselves with others is clearly an unwise practice, and yet today the world is full of those who think that they're not so bad. Television reinforces this confused type of measurement, particularly with the current pandemonium regularly offered on what the industry calls talk shows. The content of these shows has changed greatly since the early programs of this type.

Living in a Fantasy World

On television, good is often called evil, and evil is glorified as good. This contradictory reasoning sows seeds of confusion and yields acres of depravity. After several years of being conditioned by the mentalities and rationalizations of television actors, a person could easily be led to believe that, compared to others, he just isn't the worst.

When you get to the point where you even imagine you can know and understand your own heart, you are woefully deluded, as explained in Isaiah 5:21: "Woe unto them that are wise in their own eyes, and prudent in their own sight."

When the Bible says "woe," it means "woe." If you allow your thinking to become fuzzy with worldly philosophies, it will not be long before you find yourself buried in woes, wondering what happened to your life!

The world regularly, brazenly ignores the warnings and instructions of Scripture. This is not surprising at all. What is difficult to comprehend is why the *Christian* would disregard God's precepts, statutes and principles. The Bible-reading, church-attending, born-again Christian is fully aware that God is to be feared. How does he, then, become so calloused toward and confused about the things of the Lord?

As a farmer develops calloused hands from hard work, a Christian can develop a calloused heart from laboring in sin. Every time you sacrifice your mind on the altar of a corrupt TV program, you are hardening your heart against the things of God.

Television can teach us to envy, admire or enjoy the evil while despising or rejecting the good. Having calluses on the heart is a very disabling condition for a Christian and causes a lack of power in God's work.

Making Friends With the World

Would you invite a known pervert into your home for dinner and some casual conversation? How about spending an evening with a harlot—not to engage in immoral behavior with her, but just to study her form and observe her ways for about an hour? Or maybe you'd rather just yuck it up with a bunch of guys in a bar. They would tell the crude jokes, and you'd try not to laugh, but, hey, sometimes they are funny—right?

Maybe you wouldn't want to run with this type of crowd in real life, but in the make-believe world of television, many of you already have a very sordid group of "friends." Television allows you to spend time with people you wouldn't otherwise have in your home. Over time, wickedness and degeneration become normal and even humorous to you.

This adaptation soon extends into your real life. Your flesh-and-blood friends gradually become imitations of your television "friends" as you drift further and further away from people who want to follow God and His ways. You simply seem to have more fun with worldly people and carnal Christians!

I have lost track of the number of times backslidden Christians have told me that people in the world understand them better than people in their church family. Could it be that the regular meetings with the world's TV family have caused a bit of spiritual blindness?

Few things can get you to put your head on backwards like spending time with TV "friends"!

Lower Standards

A Christian woman asked me several questions one day about dress standards. This topic causes more division than a presidential election, so I rarely discuss it unless I'm teaching on the topic or I'm questioned about it. In this case, I unintentionally made a statement that brought great indignation: "Some people have higher dress standards than others because of where they are in their walk with the Lord."

I said this without malice or accusation. I was simply making an observation and went on to explain the fundamental principle of a heart that is yielded to God.

I had no idea that my words would light such a fast fuse, but before I knew it, this woman exploded! "*Higher* standards?" she blared with a tone of amazement. "How can you say that someone has higher standards and someone else has lower standards? Why don't you just say that they have different standards?" she insisted with fervor.

Our conversation went downhill like a skier on hard-packed snow. There was no way I could soften my statement and no way she was going to accept the fact that low is low and high is high.

I had not sought to offend this woman, but because I simply spoke the truth calmly, gently and in love (and she did ask), I was labeled a legalist and cast off like a leprous rag.

Why do innocent conversations about standards deteriorate into us-versus-them boxing matches? It's really quite simple. The more time you spend observing the world and learning its ways, the more you grow to admire and want to emulate what you see.

When God was leading the Israelites into the Promised Land, He made it clear that there were certain nations that were not friendship material: "They shall not dwell in thy land, lest they make thee sin against me: for if thou serve their gods, it will surely be a snare unto thee" (Exod. 23:33). The Hivites, the Canaanites and the Hittites were potentially bad influences, so God made it clear that He disapproved of any alliances with these nations.

Sowing Seeds of Spiritual Confusion

The "Hivites, the Canaanites and the Hittites" of TV today are likewise not suitable companions for the Christian! They will give us training in ungodliness, will lead us to worship their material "gods" and will be snares to us and to our families!

The longer you dwell with the wrong influence, the more likely it is that Christians with higher standards will become a source of irritation to you and you will mistakenly confuse their standards with legalism.

The *standards vs. legalism* argument is an old one but still an often misunderstood one. Too many people are pointing fingers at their brothers and sisters in fundamental churches today and crying "legalist." I'm afraid most aren't even sure what they mean by this charge.

It is necessary to understand the difference between having high standards and being a legalist. A Christian who maintains high standards based on the Word of God is simply living out his or her convictions. This is not legalism; it is just yielded obedience after salvation. Just as a growing apple tree produces apples, growing Christians will produce visible, tangible fruit in their lives. High standards are convictions that are lived out because of Christ's work in our hearts.

On the other hand, a Christian who claims that you are not saved unless you maintain a list of works is a legalist. Legalism ties salvation to a fill-in-the-blanks list of qualifying factors added to 'grace through faith.' This is far different from a person who is living out a standard from a grateful heart of love and devotion to Christ.

Light and darkness are not companions. You will not enjoy the company of Christians who are living and walking in the light when you are wallowing in the dark mud of the world. It will become increasingly easy for you to find fault with those who want to please God, if you saturate your heart and mind with the contrary lifestyles found in the average TV sitcom or drama.

Make no mistake about it—the world has a lower standard of living than God intends for a Christian to have. There are and always will be higher standards and lower standards, just as there are higher mountains and lower ones.

You will become confused if wrong information is the steady diet for your mind.

Enemies of God

How does a Christian become an enemy of God?

It is sadly simple: "Whosoever therefore will be a friend of the world is the enemy of God" (Jas. 4:4). Follow the enemy, and in effect you switch sides, making the enemy your friend and your Friend an enemy.

A Christian who talks the talk but doesn't walk the walk is a great pretender but no friend of God. "This people draweth nigh unto me with their mouth, and honoureth me with their lips; but their heart is far from me" (Matt. 15:8).

Satan, the true enemy of God, is actively making disciples through any vehicle possible. Television is the preferred appliance of the enemy because it is still considered acceptable to watch TV. While Christians can never lose their salvation, they *can* live unproductive, carnal Christian lives that would put them in direct opposition to the Saviour who died for them.

Always remember that your mind readily accepts the information that you feed it, whether good or bad. With television, images are being beamed into your mind which will then be present at a later time, whether or not you want them there. Thus, something you watch on TV *now* could cause you to resent, resist or reject the precepts and principles of Scripture *later.*

If all the information being beamed into our brains were good, then we would have no cause for concern. Unfortunately,

Sowing Seeds of Spiritual Confusion

the pictures from the average TV show, along with the dialogue, often make a disastrous impact on our understanding and our common sense.

If you insist on clinging to improper, unrestricted television viewing habits, you will find yourself one day struggling with Scripture at best, rejecting God's Word entirely at worst. Formerly held scriptural principles will come into question as you rearrange the furniture of your mind to accommodate your adjusted (distorted) view of right and wrong.

Television is a trainer, but it is not God's trainer. The "prince of the power of the air" has great control of the mass media, and television is one of his greatest tools for spreading corruption and disorder. By using repetition and saturation, the enemy is able to convince even some believers to abandon godly living and to embrace sinful lifestyles instead.

This phenomenon is clearly explained to us in I Corinthians 15:33: "Be not deceived: evil communications corrupt good manners." The "evil communications" of sitcoms, TV movies, talk shows, reality-based police shows and other dramas will eventually lead to spiritual corruption in our minds, then in our hearts, and finally in our way of living.

Has the preaching of the Word of God become irritating to you lately? Do you get tired of hearing about standards and wish the pastor would just keep his nose out of your private life? Do you find yourself disliking, avoiding or even mocking those who are striving to live for Christ? If so, you are on a slippery slope, and you'd better grab the next tree branch to stop your downhill slide before it's too late!

Spiritual confusion is life threatening. You must make a decision today to set some firm, unbendable television viewing standards before your mind becomes so confused that you are unable to think spiritually.

Is a television show really worth damaging your relationship with God?

Think about it: What do you think concerns God more: the fact that we watch things on TV that we shouldn't or that it doesn't bother us to do so?

Trap Six
Developmental Problems in Young Children

"The rod and reproof give wisdom: but a child left to himself bringeth his mother to shame."—Prov. 29:15.

Several years ago when our oldest son, Austen, was in elementary school, we went shopping at a shoe store for some gym shoes for his constantly growing feet. We hadn't been in the store for very long before we heard shouting coming from the back of the store. It was a child's voice, and he sounded very upset and seemed to want everyone to know it!

As the disturbance continued, followed by a strained reply from a woman's voice, we came to understand that this was an argument over shoes. The boy, who appeared to be around ten years old, was angry because his mom wouldn't allow him to have a certain type of shoe. The boy was determined to have his way by yelling his mom into submission.

"I want these shoes, and you're going to buy them!" the boy shouted as if he were talking to her across a football field.

The store personnel looked concerned but unsure what to do about the situation.

We selected Austen's gym shoes quickly and headed for the cash register to pay and get out of there!

As I was writing the check, the scene got worse. The boy

started swatting at the woman who we had assumed by now was his mom, and then he threw the shoes to the floor. The bellowing escalated, the store staff cringed, and the whole situation continued to spiral out of control.

Austen and I didn't stick around long enough to see how it all worked out. We couldn't leave that store fast enough!

When we got in the car, I looked over at our son, and he looked sad. "Mom, why did that boy act like that?" he asked with sincere concern and genuine puzzlement.

I gave him what has become one of my stock answers for trying to explain things that I don't always fully understand: "Honey, I'm not sure of their whole situation, but it looks like at least part of the problem is a lack of training or the wrong kind of training."

We then went on to discuss how one day, if the Lord gave him a wife and a family, it would be *his* responsibility to train his children in both what to do and what not to do.

That little boy lacked far more than basic training, but I wouldn't be surprised if another contributing factor was an overdose of television, complete with advertising designed to train him to want a particular type and only a particular type of shoes. In a way, it is actually more accurate to say that this boy was well trained!

An article in *Family Circle* magazine by Dr. Barbara Brock stated an interesting fact: in America, "more and more children are being raised by machines." Clearly, machines are not designed to do the job that parents were meant to do.

There is an epidemic of out-of-control children in our society today. You see them everywhere, from grocery stores to shoe stores, restaurants to wedding receptions, classrooms to churches. The adults in their lives are so frightened by their explosive outbursts that they become hostages trapped in a war of wills and unpredictable behaviors.

This is not what God meant when He instructed us to "train up a child in the way he should go"!

Saturation Advertising

Advertisers see our children as easy prey. They have coined a phrase called the "nag factor," which means that the advertisers will simply drench our children in ads for toys, clothes, junk food and more until they come to us and nag us into buying the latest *unneeded* item.

This tactic has been extremely successful, yielding a generation of children who cannot imagine coming out of a store empty-handed, followed by parents who will buy beyond their means, if necessary, to appease their little nagging charges.

Would you like to have more money without getting an extra job? Cut down on your child's TV time, and you won't be nagged into spending!

Many of today's toys are useless pieces of plastic that end up tossed in a corner within days of receiving them. These toys are often ridiculously priced, but they provide very little in satisfying play. A box of multicolored wooden blocks is hard to come by these days, since these simpler toys, which encourage thinking and motor skills, have been usurped by electronic gizmos, noisy motorized junk and video games. The result is a generation of children who don't know how to go out and play!

Three or four months prior to Christmas, toy retailers turn up the heat under children who watch TV. These retailers are so confident of their ability to lure your children that they spare no expense on the holiday season ads. As one toy analyst put it, "Historically, parents continue to spend money on kids even in difficult economic times."

Ten Traps of Television

Television and toy retailers work in tandem, pounding us with ads to be sure that we come out to spend money, even if we don't have any!

Newspapers throw in their two cents' worth, often reporting on the sales of the most popular toys and adding the "news" of a possible "hot" toy shortage, virtually guaranteeing that parents will shop early in a panic.

Since many of the popular toys are often mere movie or book endorsements, children are drawn to both the toy and the movie or book being promoted by the toy. This can cause a conflict for parents who would prefer not to have their children view a certain movie but are being asked to buy the related toy.

For example, many feel that the Harry Potter series is not for them or their families; but after seeing the toy ads, their youngsters want a Harry action figure. After enough exposure to the ads, a child becomes convinced that he would be the only one who didn't have a set of Harry Potter trading cards.

Can you see how this toy mania can quickly spiral downward?

Junk Masquerading as Food

The fast-food and packaged-food industries have made billions of dollars at the expense of American health, but their favorite target is the child sitting in front of the cartoons after school. Think of all the food inventions that exist merely because the advertisers have built a demand for them by parading them in front of our unsuspecting children! Who would have ever wanted a fruit snack which closely resembles plastic if it weren't for clever and manipulative advertising?

Overpriced, chemically laden breakfast cereals are another marketing phenomenon. The cereal aisle in most grocery stores is full of anything but real cereal. Toaster pastries, snack bars and sugar-encrusted boxes of puffs are the norm. Plain old

Developmental Problems in Young Children

wholesome oatmeal, a real cereal, has been relegated to a tiny section of the cereal shelves.

Other so-called food items are so full of sugar, salt and other stimulating preservatives that there is very little wonder that many children today are plagued with illnesses and diseases and other mysterious ailments previously unheard of in their age groups.

When we allow advertisers to victimize our children, we pay an untold price in health and financial woes. Real food is still cheaper than processed junk and carries far fewer health risks. Instead of passing this truth along to our children, advertisers have convinced the average child that if he doesn't have the purple ketchup on his cheese-filled hot dog, he must be deprived!

Hats on Backwards, Squinting at the Sun

Have you ever seen a little boy with his hat on backwards? Notice how he has to squint to keep the sun out of his eyes, while the bill of his cap is easily casting shade over the back of his head. He learned this from two places: TV idols and other TV-contaminated young people. And to think that all he has to do is turn his hat around to make it work right!

Little girls are asking for outfits that are replicas of ones worn by female rock stars. Often these garments are skimpy, exposing the midriff and thighs or otherwise adorning a child in clothing that isn't suitable attire for a child or an adult.

Could there be a connection between the increase in child pornography and the increase in little girls' being dressed up like miniature "ladies of the night"? Perversion needs no further encouragement these days!

Boys, who used to be practically immune to fashion advertising, have taken cues from their TV counterparts, wearing oversized pants that could hold two boys, dyeing the tips of their hair for a two-toned effect, and adding jewelry to complete the look. Even if the clothing remains clearly masculine, a young man sporting the popular look of today may have hair so long and flowing that you cannot tell whether he is male or female!

Did you ever think you'd see the day when a man would want to wear earrings and a ponytail? On TV, things have gone even further now!

Studies have proven that children who watch little or no TV are less concerned about their clothing than those who are steeped in TV ads. Your children will still have personal taste, but it will be their own, not an inherited taste from some depraved Hollywood star or music video princess.

You would be amazed at how much less fashion pressure your child would experience if you would simply reduce the number of hours that he or she is exposed to TV's idea of style.

The Confusion of Multiple Standards

When the Lord was training the Israelites to train their children, He gave them instructions to saturate the children with Scripture:

"And these words, which I command thee this day, shall be in thine heart: And thou shalt teach them diligently unto thy children, and shalt talk of them when thou sittest in thine house, and when thou walkest by the way, and when thou liest down, and when thou risest up."—Deut. 6:6, 7.

What are your children learning as they sit in your house, or when they walk in the way at the mall, or when they're supposed to be lying down for bed, or when they get up first thing Saturday morning and turn on the cartoons?

God left us with a wonderful model in Scripture that still works for training children today. The trouble is, we have dra-

Developmental Problems in Young Children

matically altered the components of God's formula. Too many parents are wringing their hands today and saying, "I don't know where I went wrong!" Could it be a training issue? Is it possible that you have corrupted the training process with too much or the wrong kind of television?

Children are very astute observers. They watch and learn and, unless hampered by a disability, are able to comprehend quickly what is acceptable and what is not.

Imagine how confusing it is for the young Christian child today who learns one set of values at church and then goes home to a contradictory set of values! Certain types of television programs are capable of breeding hypocrisy in both adults and children.

America's children are watching enough television to contaminate them for the rest of their lives. According to Dr. Jan Allen, a professor of child and family studies, only fourteen percent of the programming on television is for children, while most of what they watch is for adults. Another statistic shows that American children spend more time watching TV than they do in school! Just ask any teacher about his or her students' inability to learn grammar rules, while these same students have memorized entire TV commercials.

With the average American child watching up to twenty-seven hours of TV each week, it is easy to see that children today are being programmed. The questions are, By whom? and, In what way?

Have you watched how children play lately? The television-influenced child often "transforms" into some type of violent character or superhero, which then requires hyperaggressive forms of play that often end in someone's getting hurt.

Playground monitors have more information on this than

researchers, as these monitors stand daily on the sidelines, waiting to break up the latest imitation of an act that a child learned from his after-school hours in front of the TV.

Parents are also paying a heavy price for the generous allowance of TV time. Children, especially the very young, have a much tougher time differentiating between fantasy and reality. We may assume that they know that the characters on TV are make-believe, but many don't automatically see it that way. When a child sees another person, child or adult, engaging in some sort of behavior on TV (often without consequence), he may believe that he can do the same!

What a shame it is that parents are disciplining a child for misbehaving and then setting that same child in front of the TV for hours of misbehavior training! When you expose your child to folly and uncontrolled slapstick, you have sent your child to several hours of "fool school." Why, then, would you give the rod of correction to a child whom *you trained* to misbehave?

Just as children often *learn* readily and easily, they are also easily *confused.* You cannot "talk-teach" them one thing while regularly exposing them to the contrary without confusion and eventual bitterness.

One of the key reasons we have so many children with behavioral problems today is that we have 'provoked them to wrath' by rearing them in the nurture and admonition of television rather than in the "nurture and admonition of the Lord" (Eph. 6:4).

Face it: Television programs can be confusing and do have the capacity to teach a wrong way of living. Allowing your children to watch without supervision or specified viewing standards is a classic example of "Do as we say, not as you see."

Learning to Say and Do the Wrong Things

Children are sponges. We can fill them up, and they will

Developmental Problems in Young Children

wring themselves out and come back for more. If these "sponges" are full of television antics, then they will wring out words or actions that are crude, disrespectful or even alarming. There is nothing amazing about this predictable cause-and-effect relationship.

Years ago when our children were still in elementary school, one of them told me a dirty joke as we were driving home from school. All three of our children laughed at the punch line, until they saw the displeased look on my face. "Where did you hear *that?*" I asked in my Mom-is-not-amused tone of voice. "So-and-so told me during recess," our child replied with a perplexed look.

This was back when our children, who are home-schooled now, were in our church Christian school. This was certainly not the fault of our Christian school but could be directly traced to the home of a child in the school.

We can't begin to comprehend how difficult it is today for Christian educators to handle children who are coming from so many different parental mind-sets! We are definitely not all on the same page in Christian homes anymore.

After carefully explaining the reasons why the joke was inappropriate (which was about as easy as climbing Mount Everest—the joke was X-rated), I wondered where the original joke teller at school had heard such a thing. It sounded like Hollywood humor to my ears. In other words, somehow this child had learned to say something that was the exact opposite of what her parents would have wanted her ever to say or even know. Could this have been the product of perversion training from some after-dinner television program?

Has your child ever embarrassed you by using a vulgar term or phrase that you have never used in your home? Perhaps he learned the word from another child, but where did that child learn it, especially if he or she is from your church family? The Sunday school teacher is not teaching these things!

Unsupervised television is more dangerous than leaving a plugged-in chain saw on the floor in a room full of toddlers. We would never dream (I hope) of leaving our power tools in easy reach of our little ones. It would take only a few seconds for a child to have an accident involving a saw, drill or an electric screwdriver. We know better than to leave these things lying around!

Have you ever considered how equally dangerous it is for you to allow unlimited or unregulated access to your other "power tool"? When your child can pick up a remote control, push a button and start feeding on the swill of the world for hours, you have left him open to serious injury. Children will practice what they have learned on television, just like they practice penmanship on the paper with the wide, dotted lines.

Children who watch the average amount of TV are regularly introduced to electronic peers who think they are smarter than their parents and who have no problem smarting off to prove it. With the increase of these "family" shows, children become acquainted with the irreverent, disrespectful and ill-mannered role models of the day. Consequently, American parents are simultaneously facing a revolt from their own children while reinforcing the revolt with TV shows depicting wrong behaviors as totally normal.

Younger children are also facing an increasing amount of sexually explicit material on TV, and they are repeating words and phrases at best, attempting to imitate sexual acts at worst. Sexual assaults by very young (elementary age) children are increasing, and it's no wonder why! As mainstream television pushes the envelope further, and as fewer adults are at home to monitor what their children are watching, we are witnessing the results of this prepubescent perversion training via an explosion of sexual exploitation and corruption of young minds.

It's a very short walk from elementary school to middle school, and even shorter from middle school to high school. If a young child continually feeds on the anti-authority, do-your-own-thing messages of television coupled with the unrefined, antisocial behaviors found there, you will find in a few short years that with the help of your TV, you have created a monster.

You will want your child to sit still in church, and he won't be able to do it because the preacher doesn't flash or blink or make funny noises like the characters on TV. You will want your child to demonstrate courtesy and respect for authority, but he will respond with disregard and defiance because, after all, the children in the land of make-believe treat the adults on TV that way and those children get away with it!

You will want your child to speak with kindness and propriety, but he will be using the vernacular of the world, complete with gross phrases, slang terms and other deviant forms of speech. As you continue to try to train your child in what is right and proper, he or she will become increasingly resistant and even ultimately rebellious to your efforts.

Training up a child "in the way he should go," as Scripture instructs us, will be far more complex if you are placing him in front of a television set where he will promptly unlearn all you have tried to teach and train him to do. You are doubling your workload and rendering your child-rearing efforts unproductive and ineffectual.

Setting Up Your Child for Academic Trouble

Proverbs 23:12 advises a student, "Apply thine heart unto instruction, and thine ears to the words of knowledge." This is an excellent verse to frame and hang on any classroom wall. In fact, maybe if it were hung on the wall beside the television at home people would be more discerning in their viewing choices, especially for their children.

Teachers can usually tell you which of their students watch too much TV. The heavy TV viewers have a harder time paying attention for longer than a few seconds, unless, of course, the teacher pops a video into a VCR! In addition to their hampered attention spans, the television-addicted students tend to make more noise than the other children, often imitating commercials, theme songs and a variety of assorted sound effects.

Teachers find ways to work with and around these problems, but a more serious dilemma is posed by the fact that these children often suffer a great deal in their ability to progress academically.

According to statistics from LimiTV.org, "academic achievement drops sharply for children who watch more than 10 hours a week of TV, or an average of two hours per day."

Since the after-school time period is targeted at school-aged children, many are easily spending two hours per weekday in front of the TV, with an additional two to four hours watching the Saturday cartoons. Exceeding the ten-hour limit is an effortless job for the child who has little or no TV viewing restrictions.

The studies that have been done on television and its effect on the brain of a child are numerous, but it is not necessary to itemize and dissect each study when we can see the effects firsthand. We are watching the TV generation grow up before our eyes, and the outcome is sadly unattractive.

Part of the problem with television viewing and children is the perspective of the parents. Many parents are lukewarm about the spiritual development of their children. You could sound all the warning bells you want, but they simply won't be moved by the threat of their children's failing to bring glory to the Lord with their lives if allowed to view unrestricted TV. But if you tell a parent that his children may not achieve academic heights, well, now, you're goading the wrong ox!

How sad it is that we place so much emphasis on academic achievement but so little on godly character and development of moral excellence. If you would rather see your child earn a scholastic accolade than a Bible memorization award, you may need to reevaluate your goals and vision for him in light of Scripture. Even so, the lack of academic achievement is still an area with which we must be concerned, as reading, writing and basic math skills are necessary. If it takes the threat of poor academic accomplishment to cause parents to limit or eliminate the hours wasted in front of the TV, this is still a preferable outcome.

Draining the Brain

The problems with TV and your child's brain are multiple, so we will look at just a few.

First, the obvious problem is the impaired attention span. Since watching TV is a passive activity, children eventually become accustomed to using very little of their brains and are often resistant to efforts to make them work at learning. Why read a book when you can watch a video about the book? The TV-dependent child wants information fed to him in brightly colored, flashing and constantly changing pictures, preferably with a lively musical soundtrack!

This limited attention span doesn't go away. In fact, many colleges are finding it necessary to use videos and other forms of media stimulants in their classes in order to hold the attention of their TV-dependent students. Fewer and fewer students are able to follow simple instructions, listen to lectures or digest reading materials.

Ten Traps of Television

A second problem for the young learner is the robbery of thinking skills. Again, with the limited amount of mental effort a child must expend to watch TV, he develops a habit of allowing the TV to think for him. In a classroom with a teacher and no TV, the child is often at a loss as to what to do because of the lack of electronic stimulus.

"I'm bored" is a common complaint with this type of student. Basic seat work becomes a Mount Everest climbing expedition for the TV-trained child.

Finally, certain types of TV encourage the development of aggressive or even violent behavior in children. Have you ever seen a child lose his temper in what seemed to be an undue manner? This ability to blow up with little or no provocation has been directly linked to television viewing habits. Children who watch several hours of TV per day are exposed to countless numbers of violent acts which are stored in the mind as training exercises for dealing with life's minor irritations.

There certainly are no academic achievement awards for beating up one's peers or shouting at the teacher, but there are plenty of *demerits* for such behavior! Children who are easily angered by every petty offense that interrupts their lives are not going to be *outstanding in the classroom;* they will be *out standing by the principal's office!*

In a 1972 surgeon general's report, researchers concluded that "TV violence has serious consequences for children, making a child more willing to respond with aggression in a conflict situation, more willing to harm others and more aggressive in his or her play." These viewing habits were also linked to continuing antisocial behaviors later in life.

The Bible twice tells us, "A prudent man foreseeth the evil, and hideth himself: but the simple pass on, and are punished" (Prov. 22:3; 27:12). Do we really need researchers to do studies and conduct surveys for us before we comprehend the obvious potential harm of unlimited, unmonitored television viewing? Our children are already suffering from the impact of rampant decline in TV programming. What additional research is necessary?

We are the gatekeepers in our homes. It is our job to keep the harmful out, while allowing the good to come in.

It is way past time for children to be protected from the damaging effects of television, regardless of whether or not it is *currently* affecting their behavior!

Too Tired to Learn

Another obstacle to learning is fatigue, and a 1999 study in the September issue of *Pediatrics* linked a lack of sleep in children with the increase of homes that allow televisions in their children's bedrooms. Researchers in this study found that children with TV sets in their rooms were more likely to have difficulty falling asleep and more likely to wake up at night than those who didn't have TVs in their bedrooms.

In another study, researcher Barbara Brock found that a majority of children over the age of eight have TVs in their rooms. Little Junior isn't going to bed anymore. He's up watching late-night TV. Remember, only fourteen percent of the programming on television is for children, and virtually none of it is on after 9:00 P.M., so that tells us that children watching late at night are probably seeing pornography, hearing obscenities and learning from the "masters" how to live a life of indecency.

The same study in *Pediatrics* magazine found that there is a direct connection between having a TV set in a child's bedroom and increased struggles with parents over going to bed, and then problems in getting to sleep. Obviously, children who have televisions in their bedrooms also tend to watch far more than the average two hours per day.

What is all this late-night TV viewing doing to the child's life in school? Crippling it, that's what. The sleep-deprived little TV lover is coming to class ready for a nap, not ready to learn! Teachers included in the *Pediatrics* study reported that the nighttime viewing habits of these children were having a negative impact on their learning. Are people truly surprised by these results?

What was actually more surprising, at least in my research, was that parents mistakenly hoped to help their children fall asleep by putting TVs in their bedrooms! That's like trying to make an alcoholic sober by giving him a beer. Television is a stimulant, not a tranquilizer! Nightmares and other sleep disturbances are about the best a child can count on if he is falling asleep to the sights and sounds of TV.

As one researcher put it, "It's a slippery slope, and once parents place a television set in the child's bedroom, they automatically relinquish a fair amount of control."

The researcher went on to advise that parents clear the bedroom of TVs and computers and make it a place for relaxation and sleeping. Must we wait for a study to tell us this basic information? Sleeping and relaxing in the bedroom—what a novel idea!

A good question for educators to ask at the next parent-teacher conference is this: "Does your child have a television in the bedroom?" If the answer is "yes," then unless the teacher has the courage to speak up and suggest that the parents make immediate changes in that part of the child's life, the teacher can expect to continue seeing students with their heads down on their desks, fast asleep instead of learning.

Parents, this is not the teacher's area of control. We should not waste an educator's time by sending our children to school in rotten shape simply because we wanted to allow them to fall asleep by the TV.

Either we want our children to be able to learn, or we don't. If learning is the goal, then we must be responsible for making sure that they go to bed and get some real sleep.

A television does not belong in a child's room and is questionable in even an adult's bedroom!

TV Viewing and ADD/ADHD

When our parents were rearing us, they had never heard of ADD/ADHD. The rambunctious or spirited child certainly did exist, but a child who needed medical intervention because of his lack of attention span was a foreign concept.

Today, few grandparents are unfamiliar with the terms Attention Deficit Disorder and Attention Deficit Hyperactivity Disorder. If you don't know a person who has had a child diagnosed with this modern-day ill, you are rare indeed!

Research into the connection between ADD/ADHD and television is relatively new and therefore not entirely proven. You could locate dozens of research articles on the Internet on the subject, but with their limited test groups as well as short time periods of testing, the research is in its infancy at best.

In spite of this shortcoming, we must be aware and fully warned that evidence is swiftly mounting that there is a connection between abnormal brain development in young children and the amount of time a child spends viewing the rapidly changing images of TV.

Do you really want to wait until the jury comes in and finds TV guilty of damaging your child's brain, or will you be the "prudent" one mentioned in Scripture, hiding your child from potential harm?

How many warnings do we need? How many reams of

research must we peruse before we come to the conclusion that there is a connection between this relatively recent developmental problem in our children and their excessive exposure to television? I prefer not to wait for the "conclusive" reports!

When we look at children today, we must admit that they are far different in behavior, interests and abilities than we were as children. Some of the progress may be seen as good, such as the ability to operate a computer. Other forms of "progress" may be more accurately termed "regression" as they suffer the setbacks that accompany a mind damaged by overexposure to television.

Dr. Matthew Dumont from the Harvard Medical School made the following findings in his research on television and the hyperactive child:

1. Hyperactive behavior in children is related to the rapidly changing TV images.

2. The changing images every few seconds program a short attention span.

3. The behavior of the hyperactive child represents an attempt to recapture the flickering quality of television (LimiTV: "TV, ADD, & ADHD").

It is still too early to be able to determine conclusively the connection between television and the plague of various attention disorders. The safest route for any parent is to reduce or eliminate the risk rather than wait for the harm to be done. While studies that do suggest a connection also believe that the condition of television-induced ADD/ADHD is reversible, it would obviously be far better to practice prevention than to repair damage.

The brain is a marvelous, God-given piece of equipment unlike any other organ in our bodies. We cannot grow another one, and as of yet, medicine has not discovered a successful way to transplant a brain. Small children cannot take care of themselves, let alone protect their brains from harm. The caretaker job falls to the parents or other primary caregivers until the child is safely at an age of understanding the importance of guarding the gates of his mind.

Secret Seizures

In Mark, chapter 9, there is a fascinating story about a son that had "a dumb spirit" (Mark 9:17–29). This Scripture describes the son's condition, saying that the dumb spirit "teareth him" and that the son "foameth, and gnasheth with his teeth."

If you read this with a medical eye, it sounds like this son was plagued by seizures of some type. It is also made clear in this passage that a "spirit" or demon was behind these attacks on the son.

Jesus had the power that His disciples lacked and was able to rebuke the "dumb and deaf spirit," following it up with an instruction for that spirit to "enter no more into him." The son was finally free from the influence of the evil spirit and, hence, also free from the accompanying seizures.

Now, I am not at all suggesting that seizures from television are demon possessions, but there are some stark similarities between this story in Mark and another story reported in the news several years ago.

In fact, probably one of the most fascinating reports regarding the effects of television on the brain involved a mass seizure that took place in Japan back in 1997. While startling for just the mere fact that such a thing could happen from watching an "innocent" cartoon show, it was equally shocking in how little coverage the incident received in the news media.

This incredible lack of media coverage, coupled with an

almost nonexistent public outcry, prompted me to save the original article in my research files just in case this historical event one day mysteriously disappears from all data banks! After all, it would never do for television to have such bad press for *Pokémon*, one of the most popular cartoon characters in the history of television.

According to an Associated Press report in December of 1997, hundreds of Japanese children suffered seizures and were hospitalized after watching a vividly illustrated cartoon show on television. The program they were watching at the time of the seizures was *Pokémon*, which is a contraction for the Japanese words for "pocket monsters." The show was based on a popular video game made by the Nintendo Company.

Pause a minute to digest the previous bits of information. *Hundreds of children were hospitalized* after suffering simultaneous seizures while watching an episode of a *Pokémon* cartoon show. These children were not all together in one room but were scattered across the country of Japan, and yet they all experienced similar seizures at about the same time while watching the same program!

News reports said an explosion mixed with the strobe-light flashing of a character's eyes coincided with the viewer's epilepsy-like symptoms. A national broadcast network reported that *at least 594 people* were taken to hospitals due to the seizures.

Now you tell me, isn't this worthy of worldwide attention for at least a few weeks? If O. J. Simpson taking a slow drive down a California highway merits several days of television replays, why didn't we get at least a couple of hours of incredulous reports, follow-ups and in-depth interviews regarding the hospitalization of almost six hundred people who were sent into epileptic-like seizures by a cartoon?

An expert in epilepsy was quoted as saying that the symptoms suggested a one-time attack triggered by optical stimulus, which is different from epilepsy. This was a small comfort for those who were affected by the seizures, I'm sure. Who can be totally sure that the optical stimulus would not repeat these effects with the next exposure to a strong flash of light?

It will never cease to amaze me that such an incredible event was so neatly swept under the media's rug of image and financial protection.

Go back to the account of the son in Mark 9 where the Scripture describes the son as follows: "He fell on the ground, and wallowed foaming" (vs. 20). Now compare that picture with the one from the article about the seizure victims: "Nearly six hundred people, ages 3 to 20, suffered spasms and nausea about 20 minutes into the popular Tuesday-night program."

Are these accounts coincidentally similar, or do we need to take a closer look? "Wallowed foaming" sounds a lot like "spasms and nausea." Clearly, something invaded the minds of hundreds via their television sets.

While some would say that this comparison is a stretch, I would counter that we need to be on guard, as the "adversary the devil, as a roaring lion, walketh about, seeking whom he may devour" (I Pet. 5:8). Our children are high on the "snack list" of the enemy!

Try Talking Instead of TV

Children love to talk, and they love to have the attention of someone who cares about them. Have you ever had one of your children walk into the room and start a conversation that rambled on and went every direction? When we participate in their conversations, it says, "I love you, and what you are saying matters to me."

Researcher Barbara Brock found that families who are TV

free have more time to talk. In fact, she found that these families spent as much as an hour per day in meaningful conversation with their children. The national average is a mere thirty-eight minutes per week! Spending thirty-eight minutes a week talking with a child amounts to less than six minutes per day. No wonder children grow up and grow away from their parents. Talking becomes a casualty in homes where the TV dominates the atmosphere.

Why did you have children? Was it so you could find as many ways as possible to avoid them until they are adults? Television robs families of valuable fellowship, training time and normal conversation. You don't have to settle for this "American way" of child rearing. It is not God's design and is therefore full of flaws and pitfalls.

Show your children how much you love them by either eliminating or greatly reducing the amount of TV in their lives. Then do something that will make the researchers adjust their statistics: go and have a meaningful conversation with your child.

We are living in extremely perilous times, and the television has simply added to this peril. Our children are not mature enough to be able to sift through the rubble offered on TV. As it has been said, we are their best TV guides. If we do our jobs correctly, our children will have little or no defilement from television. On the other hand, if we practice absentee parenting and expect them to figure out right from wrong, we run the great risk of severely damaging them, possibly for life.

Think about it: Most of today's television programs are designed to "train up a child" in the way he shouldn't go.

Trap Seven
Cultivating Rebellion and Worldliness

"Be not thou envious against evil men, neither desire to be with them. For their heart studieth destruction, and their lips talk of mischief."—Prov. 24:1, 2.

Young men with two-toned hair sticking up in spikes; young ladies with skirts to the floor and vents to the back of the thigh (if they're wearing skirts at all); both with sullen expressions, unless speaking to their look-alike peers—where are we getting the pattern for this new model of young person?

Our teens today are experiencing an identity crisis of major proportions. Look around you in your church. How many young people do you see who radiate the bright countenance of one who walks with God? How many are singing when they're supposed to sing? How many young men *willingly* have their shirts tucked in and look sharp? How many young ladies *undeniably* look feminine and modest?

There is a real infestation of worldliness in our Christian young people, and we need to get underground to look at the roots of this problem.

There is no doubt that television programming has contributed heavily to the warping of young minds, causing the average teen to desire to look and act like the reprobate inhabitants of Hollywood. While movies, home videos, music videos and other forms of modern media have also donated their efforts to this slide, the easiest access to a world of poor role models is through the TV. With the increase in the percentage of children and teens who have TVs in their bedrooms—along with computers, CD players and more—we now have young people who are "marinated" in the world's thoughts, words and deeds. Talk about training!

Imitating Stars

Proverbs 13:20 tells us that the company we keep matters a great deal: "He that walketh with wise men shall be wise: but a companion of fools shall be destroyed." Who are your young people walking with when they tune in to their favorite shows? Are they walking with the wise, or are they making themselves the companions of electronic fools?

If we take a closer look at a growing plant by digging beneath the soil to peek at the roots, we'll often discover some things about the health of that plant.

In children aged thirteen to eighteen, "root rot" can set in fairly easily. All it takes is regular doses of the wrong nutrients, and before long you have a growth problem. What God meant to be a lively, thriving stage of development has been stunted and deformed by pollution from ungodly outside sources.

How are your young child's communication skills? Does he grunt instead of greet? sulk instead of smile? When you make a request, is it carried out in slow motion, if at all? On the other hand, does he become highly animated and outgoing around his peers? This is not normal development, no matter what the world is willing to accept. Understand and recognize a low standard when you see one!

When public high school students were asked to write journalism essays, it was interesting to note that even students in

Cultivating Rebellion and Worldliness

the world who are of the world found fault with the images of today's media. One student, a high school freshman, called the messages of music videos "negative" and stated that "teens are being exposed to sex, violence, drinking and misogyny" in these popular videos.

When even the world calls dirt dirty, we are absolutely careless to expose ourselves to it willingly and knowingly!

B.U.M.'s and Harlots

I'll never forget how puzzled I was when I first saw a jacket in the store that had the large letters "B.U.M." across the back. It didn't take long to figure out that this was a new name brand at the time, but I couldn't comprehend why anyone would want to call himself or herself a bum!

It seems that clothing marketed to young people today is either sloppy to an extreme or skimpy to a point of being pornographic. In other words, the boys of the world often do look like bums, while the girls closely resemble modern-day harlots. Sometimes the young men and young ladies combine both elements, with saggy clothing and undergarments exposed!

The look of the day becomes the uniform of the carnal Christian teen. When a young person is regularly in fellowship with the role models of the world, he develops an appetite for the lifestyle that these models portray. Eventually, young people on a steady diet of TV and other popular media forms become mere shadow images of what they are watching. They look, sound and act like their media counterparts.

Why would our young ladies today want to wear clothing that exposes as much flesh as possible? Could it be that they have seen so much skin on TV that they feel overdressed if something isn't hanging out?

Where did our young men get their desire to dye the tips of their hair, wear pants three sizes too big and walk like hunched gorillas with arthritis? Do you honestly believe that television has had nothing to do with these transformations?

According to a business article in the *Minneapolis Star Tribune,* teenagers of this current generation (often referred to as "Generation Y" by advertisers), reportedly spend up to an estimated $37 billion a year on apparel, while spending an additional $23 billion on entertainment and $17 billion on food (mainly junk food). This makes young people a remarkably powerful and attractive market to advertisers. One of the easiest ways for these advertisers to reach "Gen Y-ers" is by drenching them in television commercials.

When we allow our sons and daughters to mingle with the TV crowd, we are permitting them to learn the ways and means of the heathen. God warned the Israelites against this type of pollution in Deuteronomy 11:16: "Take heed to yourselves, that your heart be not deceived, and ye turn aside, and serve other gods, and worship them."

When we fail to set television viewing standards, we are failing to "take heed" to the way that we are training our young people. If we sit idly by while they learn at the feet of the wise masters of wrong living, we run a great risk of losing their hearts to the false gods of selfish pleasure and vain pursuits. We should not be astonished when TV-trained youth are able to relate more readily to wickedness than to righteousness! Training is training, whether by default or by design.

Idiot Parent Syndrome

I haven't met any parents who have the goal of being disrespected by their children. In fact, I have often heard complaints regarding a lack of respect, but never yet one that involved the problem of too much respect!

Cultivating Rebellion and Worldliness

In the land of television, idiot parents are routinely told by their superior offspring where to go and how. In fact, these "all-knowing, all-powerful," miniature "wise" ones are so prominent that it is almost impossible not to encounter one of these smart alecks in the course of an average TV week.

Since TV parents are often simpletons, young people observing them learn to *suspect*, not *respect*, authority. This lack of esteem for authority is not limited to Mom and Dad but extends to school and church authorities as well.

TV training encourages disobedience, irreverence, rebellion and ultimately reprobation among our young people. Without the guidance of authorities, sons and daughters are exposed to evil that deadens and hardens their consciences until wickedness is a way of life.

Many parents today are intimidated by or even afraid of their own offspring. In reality, some young people *are* frightening, especially when they've been brainwashed by reprobates!

"Wherefore come out from among them, and be ye separate, saith the Lord, and touch not the unclean thing; and I will receive you" (II Cor. 6:17). Television causes us to violate this Scripture when we view things that God would call "unclean."

Adults like to think that they can handle the load of smut by utilizing their mental sifter to sort the good from the bad. It's a fallacy, but a common one. Young people, especially between the ages of thirteen and eighteen, are often incapable of resisting the temptation to take just one more look. When they're placed in the candy shop of TV, young people often can't muster the drive nor the desire to protect themselves from the disguised poisons.

With the increase in "reality TV," which is truly a misnomer in the land of unreality, there has also been a increase in shows that are more warped than ever before. One of the more recent reality shows broadcast on MTV is called *Flipped*. Perhaps by the time you read this, it will have "flipped" off the viewing schedule. One can only hope.

On this show, people get the chance to experience a different side of life. According to an article by the Associated Press, a forty-year-old mom and her seventeen-year-old daughter "flipped" roles for a day. The mom spent the day at her daughter's high school, while the daughter spent the day at the office and did her mom's usual household duties.

Shows like this must be for people who have no life at all!

What was the point of this show? According to the daughter, being "mom" for the day was "horrible." On the "flip side," the mom found that math in high school was "very stressful." In the end, mother and daughter came away from the experience with a proclaimed better understanding of each other.

The unspoken accomplishments include, but are not limited to, the following: a lowering of the security for the teen as her mom masquerades as a peer, a reduction in the effectiveness of the parental authority of the mom who spent her day pretending to be her daughter, and an overall blurring of the line between adult and child.

What happens to the relationship between parents and children when television characters are frequent visitors in the home? Busy teens, who in most cases already have divided loyalties due to the vast number of hours spent with peers, are often driven further away as television peers give the deceptive impression that it is impossible to get along with one's parents. The heart of a TV-influenced teen is more easily drawn away from parents, especially if that young person is already heavily peer-dependent as well.

In Proverbs 23:26 the father pleads, "My son, give me thine heart, and let thine eyes observe my ways." While parents today would still want the hearts of their children, the world is also clamoring for this precious ground. The peers are saying, "My friend, give me thine heart." The boss at work is saying, "My employee, give me thine heart." The television friends are bidding for the remaining morsel of that heart!

We are losing the hearts of our young people today, and in many cases we are contributing to the loss ourselves. If you care at all about your young people, you must directly control their access to the TV. Unlimited access spells disaster and could cost you far more than you are willing or able to pay.

Ask yourself this question the next time your teen stalks by to turn on the TV without uttering a word: "Do I really want to train, sustain and live with a rebel?"

Lifestyles of the Rich and Foolish

I happened to overhear a conversation between two Christian young men in the school lunchroom several years ago as I was helping to warm lunches in the kitchen. They were discussing a young lady, and although their voices were lowered, they weren't low enough.

"Yeah, she's fine. You want me to hook you up?" asked the first young man, sounding more like a gangster in the hood than a Christian.

"Yeah, man, hook me up," answered the second young man, sounding equally vulgar. The rest of the conversation continued in this vein. I couldn't see the young lady to whom they were referring, but I felt sorry for her. Evidently these guys had plans for her!

In case you need a translator, as I often do, "hook me up" is slang for setting up a dating situation, one that often includes immorality. Even when it doesn't include corruption, the phrasing certainly indicates otherwise.

Ten Traps of Television

On television, when a young man and young lady "hook up," they often go so far out of bounds that they couldn't find their way back with a map. This type of vernacular has no place in a Christian's vocabulary, but it is all too common from the mouth of the average male teen idol.

Sensuality and fornication are portrayed as desirable, acceptable lifestyles on TV. For the television characters, any form of depravity goes. When these TV stars exit their unreal worlds and enter the real one, they have often made a shipwreck of their lives with broken marriages and countless affairs (which the Bible *still* calls adultery) and are often plagued with various sexually transmitted diseases. Remember, in the world of TV there are very few, if any, consequences for sinful behaviors; but in reality, where most of us dwell, it's payday someday.

Are your young people watching TV and dating without a chaperone? If so, you could have one of many things in your future, including, but not limited to, an unplanned pregnancy, a deadly disease or perhaps even jail time if the episode involves an underage young person. In fact, your teen could end up with all of the above!

"Can a man take fire in his bosom, and his clothes not be burned?" (Prov. 6:27). Can a young person be whipped into a sensuous frenzy by a scene on TV, then go out on a date and maintain his purity?

Young people today are experiencing pandemic disease and rampant pregnancies before marriage due to sexual immorality, yet they continue to engage in the very behaviors that bring on these afflictions. One of the reasons that today's youth are so willing to take risks with their health and their lives is that the TV teens have little or no disease, few or no pregnancies and almost nonexistent consequences for their lascivious conduct. *It* [pregnancy, disease, etc.] *can't happen to me,* thinks the naive young person who is steeped in TV unreality.

The Fox Guarding the Henhouse

It is so difficult to know what is acceptable to watch on TV that a person almost has to tiptoe into a show with one finger on the remote, prepared to abandon the program at a second's notice. Television producers and executives believe that they can help us with this problem by providing a ratings system to guide us through the murky waters of their programming. Let's just put the fox in charge of the henhouse and kiss all the chickens good-bye right now!

The main problem with the so-called ratings system is that it is based on a faulty premise. There is an assumption in the world that filth is acceptable as your age increases. This is a defective and dangerous principle that has produced multitudes of perverts who were fed pornography at an early age because it fell under an acceptable rating! Our young people today are a particular target of this type of maneuvering, but the ratings system does untold damage to young children as well.

The following is a copy of the guidelines found in our local newspaper. Similar guidelines are also listed in newspapers around the country. Consider the folly of this TV ratings system for a moment. (The notes in parentheses are my own observations):

TV Parental Guidelines

The guidelines are content-based and include suggested age categories.

1. TV-Y: Designed for a very young audience, including children from ages 2 to 6."

(TV "designed" for a two-year-old?)

2. TV-7: Designed for children age 7 and above. May

include mild physical or comedic violence, or may frighten children under the age of 7.

(A similar ratings chart included this phrase: "May be more appropriate for children who have acquired the developmental skills needed to distinguish between make-believe and reality." In other words, this is not *Mister Roger's Neighborhood*, neighbor.)

3. TV-G: General audience. Suitable for all ages. Contains little or no violence, no strong language and little or no sexual dialogue or situations.

(A cartoon video that falls under this category was loaned to us, and it contained a scene in which one animal called another animal a name that got our children into very big trouble when that name was repeated in our home! The video came highly recommended to us by some Christian friends who are aware of our uncompromising TV standards. "General audience" is definitely a matter of opinion!)

4. TV-PG: Parental guidance suggested. Contains material that parents may find unsuitable for younger children. Program contains one or more of the following: moderate violence (V), sexual situations (S), infrequent coarse language (L), or suggestive dialogue (D).

(In our home, we have given "PG" a more accurate label: "Putrid Garbage.")

5. TV-14: Parents strongly cautioned. May contain material unsuitable for children under 14 years of age. May contain sophisticated themes, sexual content, strong language and more intense violence.

(What, pray tell, is a "sophisticated theme"? Beware of Hollywood code phrases such as this. "Sophisticated" loosely translated by a thesaurus means "worldly.")

Cultivating Rebellion and Worldliness

6. TV-M: Mature audience only. May be unsuitable for children under 17. May contain mature themes, profane language, graphic violence and explicit sexual content.

(This is a very popular category among young people. Pornography coupled with violence have proven to be a one-two punch in the television and movie industries. Sadly, you wouldn't have to search too far to find a Christian young person who has viewed programs in this category.)

Allow me to have a bit of fun with this silly system. If I were to rewrite the TV ratings system, the elementary version would look like this:

1. TV–AAA: **A**cceptable for **A**ll **A**ges, but don't overdo it.
2. TV–BBB: **B**ad for all ages. **B**eware. **B**etter not turn it on.

Now isn't that an understandable system? Sadly, we will probably never see anything so simple as this because it doesn't serve the purposes of those who have a vested interest in the television industry. Anything that decreases viewership is unacceptable to the TV pushers and their sponsors!

The current ratings system is not only flawed, it lacks one major ingredient: an enforcement officer! What or who will stop a child of any age from watching a show that is rated "TV–M" if the child is alone with the remote control? In fact, the ratings have served more as a guide for *finding* smut than *avoiding* it! If Mom and Dad aren't home, who will be the TV police? If children and teens have televisions in their bedrooms behind closed doors, how will anyone know what they are watching?

Just as putting a dress on a pig doesn't make it a woman, putting generic labels on television programs doesn't make them suddenly safe. Those with a financial interest in the television industry want to appear compliant with your wishes for less violence, nudity and profanity; but instead of removing the offending material, they will gladly draw a map to "warn" you of its location.

With the help of these TV bosses, our young people now have a guarantee that a program will be both filthy and easy to find.

Christians need to get back to basics in regards to television. There is no ratings system created by worldly, godless individuals that would ever be acceptable to us. We need to set the viewing standards in our own homes, and we need to discard totally the notion that a person can view unclean material if he is past a certain age!

How much do you really love your sons and daughters? Do you love them enough to set boundaries around the television to protect them from spiritual, emotional and physical harm, or are you more concerned with being their buddy at this stage of their lives?

More than a friend, children need parents who are godly enough to call sin by its real name and to forbid admittance of electronic filth into their homes. If a young person is disobedient and defiant *today*, several hours, days and weeks of television will succeed in moving him downhill from disobedience to rebellion and ultimately to reprobation in a very short time.

The minds of our young people are at stake. Second Timothy 1:7 clearly states, "For God hath not given us the spirit of fear; but of power, and of love, and of a sound mind." Popular television programs, especially the shows targeting teens to young adults, promote unsound minds. Is this what you want for your young person—a life filled with fear of what the world thinks while having no fear of God? a replica of some Hollywood actor, but a mere shadow of a Christian?

It won't be easy to establish new rules in a home where the television has reigned supreme, but the payoff will be worth all the minor discomforts that you may encounter as your family makes the needed adjustments.

Worry more about what God thinks of how you are raising your young person. You will give an account for that one day.

Think about it: "To have the home, school and church proclaiming one set of values to the child while your TV set vigorously and effectively teaches another is to cause confusion of the first order."—Ronald E. Williams, *Christians' Pet Sin.*

Trap Eight
Spoiling Christians in Their Later Years

"The hoary head is a crown of glory, if it be found in the way of righteousness."—Prov. 16:31.

On Tuesday, September 11, 2001, two airliners plowed into the World Trade Center. Later, another civilian airliner crashed into the Pentagon. On the same shocking day, yet another aircraft slammed to the earth in rural Pennsylvania. These crashes were all attributed to a calculated terrorist attack on America in which thousands of lives were lost and the security of our nation was changed forever.

My mother, who was on vacation in Florida at the time, phoned to tell me that an airplane had hit the World Trade Center where my older sister worked. As soon as I hung up the phone it rang again, this time with the wife of our preacher on the phone. I told her what my mom had just told me, only to find out that Mrs. Johnson was witnessing this same thing on her TV as we spoke. We quickly ended our conversation and went to find out more about this unfolding drama.

Since our TV didn't have access to network stations, we had to forage through the closet for an old black-and-white portable TV that is reserved for emergencies or extremely special events. This was a national emergency, so we dug out the little box and wiggled the antenna just in time to see the second airliner as it pummeled the second tower. Even on a small screen, the image was beyond horrifying.

By the end of the day, we had finally heard from my sister, who had been shopping before work in the main floor of one of the towers at the time of the crash. She escaped but bears emotional scars that come with surviving such a catastrophic event.

Since we home-school, our three children and I spent about an hour viewing the reports that were coming in one on top of another during the terrorist attacks on our nation. After about an hour of seeing the images of the airplanes hitting the towers, our youngest son, Collin, asked, "Why do they keep showing that same picture over and over again?" He found it appalling, and as infrequent viewers of network TV, we were all impacted not only by the images themselves, but also by the instant replays of these images. After Collin's perceptive question, we turned off the TV and went to pray.

The elderly, who are often practically hostages in front of their televisions, not only watched this horror unfold, but were also subjected to repeated film clips of the worst parts of this disaster for days and weeks to come. Graphic photos of the second aircraft smashing into one of the Twin Towers, along with footage of people running down the streets of New York City, faces twisted into masks of unmitigated fear, were replayed countless numbers of times, virtually etching the images into the minds of viewers.

As is typical in a country so accustomed to the instant availability of information through technology, Americans saw innumerable photos of these tragic multiple attacks within a week or so. For the elderly, TV is often the main window to the world in general. Seniors who use the television as a substitute companion were assaulted again and again with images of one of the most mournful events in our nation's history, making this world seem more frightening and hideous than we could imagine.

TV Addiction Is Prevalent Among the Elderly

Visit just about any nursing home during the day or evening, and you will find not one but several televisions going at the same time, even if they're located in the same room. Not only are TVs used for background noise, they are also used as a surrogate for human contact. Loneliness and a sense of isolation develop in spite of the constant company from TV characters.

Television is a poor replacement for communicating with real people. Hours of talk shows, game shows, soap operas and sitcoms are to the mind what fast-food restaurants are to the body—pure junk, which eventually take a toll on health and well-being.

In addition to the loneliness, there is the sense of greater unreality that develops from spending so much time in the land of make-believe called television. How long will it be before we are hearing about studies pointing to TV as a possible trigger in various forms of dementia and other mind-related illnesses? I don't think we want to risk waiting for another research paper to be written! Our elderly are suffering, and television isn't helping them one bit.

Fear for Sale

While advertisers view the elderly as a wonderful target market for drugs and other medical products, television producers view them as a group of "eyeballs" who will watch almost anything—hence the glut of daytime dramas and senseless drivel found on talk and game shows.

One of the cruelest consequences of so many hours in front of the TV is that it breeds an overwhelming sense of fear and hopelessness in the life of an elderly viewer. Trapped in front of the TV for eight to twelve hours, people can become extremely jaded and fearfully warped in their view of life in this world.

Constant bombardment of violent, frightening images can push fears to incredibly abnormal heights, causing some of our elderly loved ones to avoid even basic daily activities such as taking a walk in the neighborhood or shopping for groceries at the local store. Some of our elderly feel that there is no safe place outside of their homes or apartments, and this idea has been greatly nurtured by television.

Crippling Effects

In addition to crippling the elderly through inflated fear, the "prince of the power of the air" uses TV to disable our older loved ones through lack of physical activity. Television is a passive activity, with even the brain settling into a receive-only mode of operation. Health problems, as well as mobility problems, are made worse by the hours of sitting, virtually locked in a chair. Instead of getting outdoors in the fresh air for a stroll or exercising the mind in other more positive and stimulating ways, people sit and stare at a TV, producing a self-inflicted state of complete lethargy.

If you are in your "autumn years" and reading this, please beware. You are desired by an industry that would rob you of your health and then try to sell it back to you in the form of a drug or device. You are a target and are only as valuable to the television industry as your wallet or your checkbook. The TV tycoons don't care about you, but they would love to have a look at your money!

We need our elderly loved ones more than ever. This society has made every task that we do more confusing, confounding and filled with traps at every turn. The wisdom that comes from the "hoary head" could make an enormous difference in the outcome of the next generation. If our elderly are all ailing, trapped in nursing homes and sitting mesmerized in front of the TV, we will lose one of our greatest national treasures.

Spoiling Christians in Their Later Years

If you have elderly parents or grandparents who show signs of being addicted to TV, one of the best things that you could do for them would be to spend more time with them. People watch less TV when they have regular interaction with the real world. Provide rides to church, the doctor or the store. Include them in your ministries or other activities in which you can interest them.

Many seniors today feel abandoned and forgotten. If your older family members are watching too much TV because everyone else is too busy for them, plan a way to change that—and soon.

The enemy knows that "in the multitude of counsellors there is safety." We can't sit back and allow our seasoned counselors to be idled on the sidelines. The "safety" that their wisdom and counsel provide is too valuable to be squandered on the altar of TV. Instead, let's disable the power that TV has in their lives by providing loving companionship, genuine care and availability without being called or asked.

If you are a senior, please consider how much you are needed for your wisdom and guidance. You are a treasure from God. Don't allow the enemy to squander your health, finances and spiritual well-being through the hypnotism of television.

Without your aid and involvement, families and ministries will not be all that they could be, as God intended for those with the "hoary head" to help lead others in the way God wants them to go.

Beware of the enemy's attempt to disarm and disable you!

Think about it: A great way to cripple America is to incapacitate her senior citizens. Frighten them, drug them, crowd them into care facilities—do anything to keep them from positively impacting the next generation with their wisdom, and America as a whole loses strength in the end.

Trap Nine
Marriage Pollution

"Wives, submit yourselves unto your own husbands, as it is fit in the Lord. Husbands, love your wives, and be not bitter against them."—Col. 3:18, 19.

Have you watched anything on TV lately that has had a sensually stimulating effect on you? Perhaps it began as just an innocent time of channel surfing when suddenly you accidentally stumbled upon what the industry refers to as soft porn, also known as any average underwear commercial these days. No matter what you were watching, the bigger question is: What was your response after you realized you were in Smut Land? Did you attempt to flee by swiftly changing the channel, or did you linger and look?

We are facing an epidemic of divorce among Christian couples. Does television have anything to do with this? Research in this area is difficult to find, but it is enough for the discerning Christian to know that when we contaminate ourselves with the wicked *ways*, *thoughts* and *social values* of this heathen generation, we are going to suffer from their *afflictions* as well.

This reminds me of the time my husband had a bad cold. He coughed most of the night, and after sharing the same room with him, it took me three days to catch my own version of his cold. When Christians immerse themselves in the world's philosophies for marriage, they wake up with the world's marriage problems.

Pornographic Problems

Many people become addicted to hard-core pornography by being fed smaller doses of the equally poisonous, so-called soft porn. Soft or hard, there is no difference to God. Sin, whether soft or hard, is still sin. Nakedness, whether full or partial, is still nakedness.

Remember Noah? In Genesis 9, we find the account of Noah's getting drunk on the wine from his new vineyard. Noah was a righteous man, but he clearly had a lapse in judgment here, ended up in a drunken stupor and "was uncovered within his tent" (vs. 21). Noah's son Ham went in and looked at his father's nakedness; then instead of covering him, he broadcasted his father's shameful condition to his brothers.

Notice in verse 23 the dramatically different response of Ham's brothers, Shem and Japheth:

"And Shem and Japheth took a garment, and laid it upon both their shoulders, and went backward, and covered the nakedness of their father; and their faces were backward, and they saw not their father's nakedness."

The story ends with Noah's waking up and finding out what Ham had done and declaring a curse upon Ham's descendants through the lineage of his son, Canaan. Shem and Japheth, on the other hand, had Noah's blessing bestowed upon them.

If Ham had had more integrity, he would have reacted correctly. His brothers obviously knew and immediately understood the sin of even looking on their father's nakedness, and they protected their eyes by walking into their father's tent backwards. Shem and Japheth displayed discretion and respect for their father.

We must likewise shield ourselves from illicit images that are so readily available in television programs and commercials. If you watch something sensual on TV, face it—"to him that knoweth to do good, and doeth it not, to him it is sin" (Jas. 4:17).

Dr. Ross Olson, a pediatric physician with Health Partners in Minnesota, has written on many topics, including the issue of pornography. In his research paper titled "What's Wrong With Pornography," he makes this valid point: "Sexual behavior is very highly rationalized—people are capable of justifying anything they really want to do. Just as it is not sensible to try crack cocaine just to see what it is like, the wisest answer to pornography is just to say never."

From Seeds of Lust to Weeds of Discontentment

"I just don't love her anymore. She doesn't turn me on."

"I just don't love him anymore. He's so unromantic."

"She's lost her looks."

"He's lost his drive."

On and on the sad laments go. People are leaving their spouses for weaker reasons and in greater numbers than ever before in our history. At the same time, television continues to portray unhealthy, perverted and adulterous relationships as the desirable norm, while making marriage seem like some ancient form of bondage. In a television interview one popular singer said, "Marriage is an institution. Why would I want to live in an institution?"

Husband, your wife is not the harlot-actress that you see on TV. Wife, your husband is not the philandering Romeo on the soap opera. Keep comparing your spouse to those TV "ideals" long enough, and you will have very little left of your marriage! Repeated exposure to shows that portray simulated sex or sexual innuendo can breed insatiable lust and massive discontent in a marriage.

Ten Traps of Television

Who can measure up to the perfect people in TV programs? Even the TV stars themselves can't do it, and they admit it regularly in their magazine interviews. (One-year marriages are considered miracles of great length with the Hollywood crowd.)

After I had taught a workshop on the "Ten Traps of Television," a woman came up to me and said, "You left out one important part. What does a wife do when her husband watches filth on TV, but the wife doesn't want to?"

She went on to describe how her husband spends his evenings after work watching entertainment wrestling at full volume in the living room. Her children are allowed to watch it with him if they choose to, though this wife noted that her children often opted not to join Dad for his hour of fun.

A man who puts his TV preferences ahead of the well-being of his family will have a very large bill to pay one day. Even if his marriage survives, the children will be trained to believe that it is acceptable to reproduce the same type of home they grew up in. Dad may come by for a visit in the home of his adult child one day, and the TV will be on its throne in the living room, full blast and showing images that will very possibly make Dad want to blush.

Fathers, you are not bringing your children up in the nurture and admonition of the Lord when you sit and watch base and degrading shows on TV, but you *are* sending a message to your children that TV is more important than your family. Your wife gets the message loud and clear, and the future marriages of your children will yield the fruit of poor cultivation.

Wives, if your husbands watch shows that you know are inappropriate, go find something else to do, and pray for him while you're at it. There is great power in prayer, and God hears the cries of a godly wife. Keep yourself pure at all costs, then go and cry out to the Lord in fervent, earnest prayer.

In Malachi 2:13, the Lord demonstrates how He does see the tears of a wife and His ear is open to her cry: "And this have ye done again, covering the altar of the LORD with tears, with weeping, and with crying out, insomuch that he regardeth not the offering any more, or receiveth it with good will at your hand." The priests were being chastised for their mistreatment of their wives. Nothing is hidden from God!

In verse 14, God specifically accuses the priests of their sins: "The LORD hath been witness between thee and the wife of thy youth, against whom thou hast dealt treacherously: yet is she thy companion, and the wife of thy covenant."

Husbands, what would God have to say to you about how you are dealing with your wife? Are you forcing her to endure your illicit television viewing habits while expecting her to remain tender and responsive toward you? God knows all about it!

If you are a man who thinks he can handle a little nakedness, remember David. He couldn't hold up under the pressure of viewing Bathsheba's nakedness, even when viewed from an apparently long distance! You are no match for the wiles of the Devil. He will either maim you or destroy you through the "lust of the eyes" (I John 2:16).

If you are a woman who has been feeding on the fantasies of soap operas or other damaging TV dramas, beware and be warned! "A little leaven" is all it takes to raise a whole lump of discontentment in your heart (Gal. 5:9). Your husband is under no obligation to match, imitate or otherwise fulfill the false ideas that you learn from the leading men on TV. Just as you would not want to be compared with another woman, your husband does not want to compete with other men, even if those men live in Hollywood.

Ten Traps of Television

Unrealistic Expectations

Homes are cleaner on television. Days go swiftly and are more fun. People at work are good-looking. And when a man comes home, he has a fantastic-looking wife or live-in lover to wrap up his day. Oh, the fantasy life in the land of unreality!

In the meantime, back in the real world, moms struggle to keep a home neat and clean while children, who rarely value a tidy home, go behind her making new messes. Bills need to be paid. Phones need answering. Skinned knees and broken bones interrupt schedules. Days often start before sunrise and go way beyond sunset. Husbands are often under stress from jobs that might be here today and gone tomorrow. Who needs any more pressure?

Television, complete with its world of illusion, leads to unrealistic expectations in all aspects of life but particularly in the realm of marriage. Who wouldn't want to come home to someone who always has every hair in place, never has a dirty house, maintains the same body weight as a twelve-year-old girl and is witty and attentive to boot?

In addition to these *minor* fantasies, greater problems develop when the repeated displays of plastic perfection provided by television are embedded in the mind. Men today are becoming increasingly more demanding in regards to their wives' physical appearance, and if a woman doesn't measure up to today's standard of beauty, the TV-trained man can become very irritated and ungratified.

The more a man sees of the television ideal of beauty, the more his mind becomes conditioned to accept this as the only permissible norm. The more pressure that is placed on a wife to measure up, the more discord there is between spouses.

God has given us "natural affection" (Rom. 1:31), and it becomes warped and tainted when poisoned by the TV standard of affection. If we are not careful, we could find ourselves hating the ones whom God has given us to love and cherish, while lusting after ones who are on the electronic screen.

Are you pleased with your spouse lately? If not, what have you been watching on TV, and what unrealistic expectations have you been placing on your beloved? Examine yourself carefully.

Low Standards Go Lower

Every home has one spouse who has greater influence over the other. It is not always the case that the husband has the greater sway, even though he is the God-designated leader of the home. In many homes, the wife is the one who inspires—to any level from great heights to lowest depths.

Wives are so capable of influencing their husbands for good or for evil that it should be our daily prayer that we never do or say anything that may cause our husbands to be less than what God wants them to be. In the area of television, what we watch may cause them to accept even lower standards.

Men who have made covenants with God regarding their eyes are not easily swayed by anyone or anything. Men who are bent on walking with God have themselves on constant watch. Expecting the enemy to attack, they stay armed, guarded and ready to respond. Husbands who do not walk as closely with the Lord are far more vulnerable.

Wives, are you aware of your potential impact on your husbands?

In chapter 3 of the Book of I Peter are guidelines for the woman married to a man who 'obeys not the word.' This Scripture tells us that the man is "won by the conversation" of his wife. In other words, if you are a living example of godly purity, it could make a vast difference in the life of your less-than-spiritual husband.

On the other hand, if your life consists of low or double standards, the ungodly husband only becomes more tyrannical and impossible to please. Godliness in any person is attractive, while ungodliness is repulsive.

Wife, what are you watching on TV, even when your husband isn't present? Don't think that you can fool him by pretending to be Mrs. Purity when he gets home. Godliness is a lifestyle, not an article of clothing that you put on and take off at your convenience. If you've got it, you will radiate it. Without it, your words will ring as hollow as your testimony.

Contaminating the Wells of Marital Love

My husband and I have a growing list of couples for whom we pray regularly, sometimes several times a day. We are witnessing an alarming number of troubled marriages and divorces among our brothers and sisters in Christ. Even just a few Christian couples breaking up their marriages would be too many, but we are way beyond just a few!

Television did not create divorce or even the unhappy marriage. What television does is contribute to the deterioration of a marriage. If a person is ailing and you expose him to bacteria, he will face greater infection and have less fight in his system to deal with it. When you introduce filmed sensual acts, lewdness and unrealistic expectations into an already fragile marriage, what was frail becomes weaker until ultimately it is broken or destroyed.

While there are many programs on TV that are hazardous to our spiritual health, probably the most damaging are those dramas that include sexual innuendo and other pornographic situations. Don't kid yourself. A program's being on network TV rather than on cable TV doesn't make it clean! In order to compete with cable, TV promises to become viler by the season. Television executives call it pushing the envelope. It's time we pushed the envelope back to them!

Unadulterated Love

In Genesis 4:1, the Bible gives the most beautiful terminology for the intimate relationship between a man and his wife: "And Adam knew Eve his wife; and she conceived." The relationship that the world calls merely "sex" was called 'knowing' by our God. Adam "knew" Eve. God's pattern for love is so much more beautiful and meaningful than the satanic debauchery of today. Husbands and wives can still have this type of knowing-each-other relationship, but it requires a vigilance and protection against impure influences. God's plan for marital love is far more rewarding than the mere shadow image portrayed by the world.

When a husband spends too much time watching TV "babes" and their counterparts, it arouses sinful desires and stores impure images in the heart and mind. No one can deny the stimulating power of pornography, but some will *try* to deny it. God knew all about our tendencies to rationalize, so He nailed down this issue in Scripture for us:

"Ye have heard that it was said by them of old time, Thou shalt not commit adultery: But I say unto you, That whosoever looketh on a woman to lust after her hath committed adultery with her already in his heart."—Matt. 5:27, 28.

The truth is, you cannot love your spouse properly if you are allowing unclean images to corrupt your mind. 'Knowing' and loving your spouse within the safe bounds of marriage is a beautiful, bonding experience. Outside of these boundaries, depravity and selfish lust are destructive and damaging forces. Whether it is the man or the woman engaging in mental fantasies, the result is the same: adultery is being committed in the heart.

Ten Traps of Television

If you have a happy marriage, you have a gift from God. Don't risk ruining it for a few moments of artificial, electronic pleasure. If you have a troubled marriage, you can't afford the debilitating effects that television porn would have on your already fragile existence as a married couple.

Viewing sensual material feeds unnatural affection. God-given "natural affection" builds a marriage. Unnatural affection tears down a marriage.

Think about it: Perversion is pervasive. Just as weeds will choke the good plants in a garden, perversion will choke the proper development of love within a marriage.

Trap Ten
Glorifying "Strange Womanhood"

"For the lips of a strange woman drop as an honeycomb, and her mouth is smoother than oil: But her end is bitter as wormwood, sharp as a twoedged sword. Her feet go down to death; her steps take hold on hell."—Prov. 5:3–5.

People magazine has a regular issue in which they name the "sexiest person of the year." It features the latest star, usually of movies or TV, who has somehow managed to lay claim to this dubious distinction.

It always amuses me how unattractive these people appear to my media-deprived eye. The first things I often notice are that the men need haircuts and a shave and the women need more clothes and possibly a few more pounds.

What in the world is "sexiness"? And is it a desirable quality for a Christian to possess? I believe that what the world calls sexy is the same thing that the Bible calls "strange," which immediately tells me that it is not the awe-inspiring condition that the world makes it out to be. Luke 16:15 makes this issue clear: "That which is highly esteemed among men is abomination in the sight of God." Sexiness is "highly esteemed among men," but it is abhorrent to the Lord. Still, many of our women today have been corrupted with the notion that they are to be attractive to any and all men and are to stay that way until death!

Ten Traps of Television

Sexiness at Any Cost

So-called sexiness carries a high price tag. The Bible says that the end of the strange woman is "bitter as wormwood." Proverbs 7:27 says that the strange woman's "house is the way to hell, going down to the chambers of death." Not exactly what you'd call a great street address!

If you spend too much time viewing the lives of the 'strange women' of television, you will gradually desire to imitate them. If your best efforts to be a living *femme fatale* fail, you can expect bouts of lowered self-esteem because you are unable to impersonate the vixens of TV.

Very rarely does a woman look at the electronic paper dolls on TV and respond with what she should—open disgust. Hollywood has found a willing bunch of poor excuses for women who might as well stand on the street corner holding up cardboard signs that read, "Will work for fame and fortune. No food or real life required."

All Made Out of "Ticky-Tacky"

Do you remember the song from years ago where the singer told of houses that were all made of ticky-tacky and all looked alike? I am reminded of that song whenever I see the cover of the periodicals at the grocery store checkout line. The women on those covers look suspiciously alike!

It is no accident that so many women today seem to look related to one another. TV is very effective at training women to adopt a certain image and then to parade that image in front of anyone who will look. In most cases, since so many of the TV actresses play the roles of liberated women, the imitators are trying desperately to achieve the same, artificial lifestyle that they're seeing on TV. Somebody needs to clue a few people in that TV IS NOT REAL!

Glorifying 'Strange Womanhood'

In addition to becoming cookie-cutter women in their appearance, there is the related problem of women carelessly desiring and aiming to gain the attention of men other than their husbands. In an effort to imitate the potent wiles of their TV models, these women use body language, wear provocatively fitted or revealing styles of clothing and employ any other tools that will get a man to look twice.

If the man is not careful in guarding his eye gates, he could find himself lusting after this type of woman and even committing adultery with her in his heart, if not in real life! This type of dangerous game can ruin marriages.

Lust Promotion

Women portrayed on daytime soap operas as well as evening sitcoms and dramas have one thing in common: they appear to be without spot or wrinkle, bump or lump. The latest acceptable female form closely resembles something like a coat hanger, but as long as the media says it is the desirable look, women across America are busy either trying to achieve it or lamenting their inability to do so.

Isn't it interesting that the so-called sexy woman on TV rarely possesses any quality other than her physical appearance?

The enemy has been working overtime to breed massive discontentment among wives and husbands. Lust on TV is a spectator sport which sends a clear message to female viewers that they'd better provide something worth lusting after. A godly, pure and discreet woman is virtually nonexistent in the world of television (except when needed for scorn or ridicule), while the TV harlot has been elevated to a pedestal status that no ordinary woman could attain. For those with eyes to see, what we are really witnessing is Scripture brought to life: "As a jewel of gold in a swine's snout, so is a fair woman which is without discretion" (Prov. 11:22).

Ten Traps of Television

In desperation due to repeated exposure, the Christian woman could be led to compete with her TV model. This vain pursuit of good looks often jumps ahead of one's quest for holiness and Christian character.

It is the "gracious woman" of the Bible that "retaineth honour" (Prov. 11:16), not the harlot! As the competition escalates between the TV woman and the real woman, the spiritual condition declines, eventually leaving a woman drained and unfulfilled. Younger women look on in horror, wondering how they might escape the fate they see befalling their older, supposed role models.

In her book, *Hunger Pains,* Dr. Mary Pipher described how one of her clients views the world in which women live today: "In this society, you have to be pretty first; then you can think about having character, being smart and achieving things. If you aren't pretty, nothing else matters." As Dr. Pipher observed, "To be a woman is to have a body-image problem. For so many of us, thinness equals attraction, which equals value."

What a sad commentary on the value of women "in this society." Television reinforces this distorted belief by continuously choosing the ultrathin, unrealistically airbrushed beauty and displaying her before the world as perfection personified. Of course, once this female picture of perfection starts to age, get wrinkles or gain a pound or five, she is no longer their beauty queen.

It is an unworthy purpose in life to attempt to compete with the images promoted on TV. No matter how good the television actresses may look electronically, they have to take off all that "powder and paint that make a woman what she ain't"; and when they eventually do, they have very little else to offer. As my grandma used to say, "Pretty package, nothing inside." Is that really how you want to be remembered?

Glorifying 'Strange Womanhood'

Strange Women Make Strange Mothers

I was standing in line at the grocery store one day when I saw two women who looked like they could be sisters, except that one of them had a decidedly older face. They were wearing the same type of clothing, sporting the same hairstyles, wearing matching makeup; but one of them definitely had a few more years on her driver's license. From the back, they looked like a pair of teenage girls, complete with tight jeans, black leather jackets and hair that looked like they had just come out of a windstorm.

Imagine my surprise when I heard the younger say, "Mom, did we remember the...?"

Mom? She looked more like a teen who grew old and forgot to change her clothes!

Does television have anything to do with this new wave of adult women who are striving to look like teens? Well, you do the math. We have two groups that create this problem: television writers and producers who want to perpetuate a myth that real women never grow old, and advertisers who prey on the weakness of women who never feel adequate, beautiful or young enough. Add them together, and you have both impact and influence.

A September 1999 article in *USA Today* told about the show on Fox TV called *Get Real*. The newspaper article included a photo of the actresses who were playing mother and daughter. Guess what. They were dressed alike—daughter in tight jeans and a T-shirt that looked like it had been through the dryer on the "shrink cycle"; mother in matching outfit! In the photo they were sitting on the edge of the daughter's bed, and at a glance, you would be hard-pressed to determine who was in charge.

What is this like-daughter-like-mother syndrome doing to our young ladies? What kind of message is it sending? How can a young girl, in the throes of the raging of her own hormones, accept a mother who is approaching menopause and dressing like a "teenybopper"?

Many people today refuse to accept the messages that clothing can potentially send, but evidence speaks for itself. Parents today are having pandemic problems maintaining any level of authority over the young people in their homes. Could it be possible that the young people are having a very tough time submitting to someone who looks like a child?

On a recent trip to a local warehouse store, I saw another "hybrid momteen" shopping with two small boys and what seemed to be her husband. Once again, the clothing screamed, "I am a former teenage rebel, and I'm proud of my too-small shirt and my too-tight jeans because at least I was able to squeeze into this rig!"

At one point, her younger boy was trying to get her attention, while she was talking loudly enough to the cashier to get everyone else's attention (which appeared to be the goal). Her husband just stood there and shuffled around a bit. "Mommy, Mommy," the little boy repeated several times, until finally he grabbed the belt loop of her low-slung jeans and gave it a firm tug. That got her attention!

Her follow-up response was clamorous, tense and abnormal. I felt sorry for the little guy, because what he really seemed to need was a full-grown mommy, and what he seemed to have was a grown woman who was acting like a toddler.

Could it be that the television ideal for the beautiful woman has reached such ridiculous heights as to convince a large portion of the female population that they must look like children?

It is more than possible; it is probable, and the evidence is all around us in public. Women certainly aren't just conjuring up these images in their heads!

Glorifying 'Strange Womanhood'

Our children need adults who look, act and think like adults. If they can't find any, then peers will have to do.

Christian mother, you may look young because it runs in your family, but there comes a time in life when there needs to be a definite difference between you and a younger woman. We are to be patterns of the godly, gracious woman, not replicas of the strange women of the world. If you have been playing this look-alike game, consider your ways. You will impact other young ladies around you. What type of impact do you want to have?

A Stranger Wife

"Foolish" and "clamorous" is the description of the strange woman in Proverbs 9:13. In fact, verses 13 to 18 make an excellent example of the antithesis of a gracious woman. Every Christian mother who has a daughter ought to spend some time discussing this passage as an outline of what *not* to be as a woman. Foolish and clamorous women make spectacles of themselves, and they don't make good wives.

Sadly, "foolish" and "clamorous" are in style today. Women who are television-trained are making more noise in public than ever before. We are getting to the point where hearing aids may soon become unnecessary! What is all the noise about? It is a thinly veiled attempt to get more attention. By talking more loudly, laughing more boisterously and generally making a scene, the clamorous woman is actually saying, "Pay attention to *me!*"

Christian wives who play this game are both poor examples and dangerous. I know that there are countless Christian women (and likely even unsaved women) who feel about their husbands as I do about mine: I emphatically do not want another woman trying to get my husband's attention!

I wonder, What would the clamorous woman do with the

attention if she were able to get it? If the intent is not adulterous, then what is it? As the coarse yet true saying goes, "If there ain't no party, then quit sending out invitations!"

If you are a Christian wife, you must firmly purpose in your heart and life never to attempt to attract the attention of another man. Then, you must carefully guard and shield your eyes from the foolish examples found on TV. You are not, and will never be, that electronic every man's woman found in the latest TV drama. Be thankful that you have a real life and live it right!

The good-looking woman easily snares many men, especially those who are steeped in media images. Let's face it, beauty can be something to behold. Beauty is also something that changes, and if there is no godly character beneath that attractiveness, a woman can plan on a barren existence in the future. A man may enjoy all the sights and noise for a season, but he will soon grow tired of a woman who wants everyone's attention—especially when she's older.

A Place of Dishonor

'Strange womanhood' is not a place of honor; it is a place of debasement, emptiness and sorrow. You may be able to get a few moments of pleasure by being an object of attraction, but eventually you will grow old and be left with superficial memories and virtually no effectiveness as a woman of God. There are, and always will be, serious consequences for toying with sin. If you have been playing the part of the sexy, attractive flirt, it is time to quit pretending and start working on your character as a godly woman.

"Favour is deceitful, and beauty is vain: but a woman that feareth the LORD, she shall be praised" (Prov. 31:30).

Appearances last for only a season. Godliness is good for a lifetime.

Glorifying 'Strange Womanhood'

Think about it: A Christian woman who tries to imitate the worldly Hollywood role model is like a beautiful flower in a bed of weeds. She doesn't belong and she can't compete; she just puts on a good show.

Chapter Eleven
A Plea to the Leader of the Home

"Turn away mine eyes from beholding vanity; and quicken thou me in thy way."—Ps. 119:37.

Years ago when our children were elementary aged and younger, I went to my husband to make a request—not a demand, but a request. You see, I had witnessed the effects of television on our children firsthand. The training that we were trying to do was being contradicted and hindered by TV. After a couple of years of seeing children's television programs going from bad to worse, I went to my husband with an appeal to eliminate network TV from the lives of our children.

I didn't even discuss our own personal TV habits, although I had already purposed in my mind that I was going to follow the same restrictions that I would be placing on our children. If network television was transforming them by the warping of their minds, it could do the same to me. Still, I knew not to suggest that my husband follow suit at that time. I was perfectly content to obtain his permission to deal with the children, and I knew that the Lord would direct my husband about his viewing choices in due season.

Even though I had gone to the trouble of preparing my case as if going before a judge in a court of law, my husband had no objections to my plan. I expected at least a look of disbelief or

Ten Traps of Television

wonder as I outlined my plan to replace their TV hours with other activities, which would include additional time spent at the library. He, perhaps as prepared by God, simply gave me the green light to begin implementing my plan to protect our children from the damaging effects of TV in their lives.

Now, it was not without a bit of fear on my part that I "dived into the deep end of the pool" with this new plan. Many stay-at-home moms are accustomed to using the TV as baby-sitter, and many of them are unwilling to give up this free in-home child care! Was I going to have to become the full-time camp counselor at home, and was that going to result in my husband's coming home to an even-more-frazzled-than-usual mother of three young children? This remained to be seen. I had to trust that the Lord would bless this effort.

I wish now that I had marked that date on the calendar, because I cannot remember how many years ago we made that life-altering decision in our home. It was at least eight or nine years ago. Regardless of how many years have passed, the point is this: we have all survived without network TV!

The television is now treated as a mere appliance which is kept on a stand that we roll in or out of the closet as needed. It is used mainly for viewing prescreened videos that are purchased, given to us as gifts or borrowed from our local library.

We also have a game unit, which is a colossal time waster if not closely monitored. Any games purchased have to meet a tough screening standard, and if they fail, they can't become a part of our game collection. We limit overall TV time (games or videos) to an hour or two on Thursdays and Fridays after school, with a few free-time hours on Saturday. On Saturday evening, the TV is rolled back into the closet, where it stays until the next appointed time. As the saying goes, "Out of sight, out of mind."

A Plea to the Leader of the Home

Why am I telling you all of this? Well, since the husband is the head of the home, it is necessary for him to be in favor of controlling the TV in order for the wife to establish an effective TV policy with the children. Most husbands delegate a great deal of the child training to their wives, and this leaves them in a very vulnerable position if they are without adequate support from "the top."

Ephesians 5:11 tells us clearly to "have no fellowship with the unfruitful works of darkness, but rather reprove them." Television places us in direct fellowship with the very works that God warned us against. We not only learn about the "unfruitful works of darkness" in great detail, but we are also encouraged to become fruitless as we waste hours in ten-minute segments of commercials. Tying it all together, we have a package of wasted time.

What do you watch on TV? Is it God-honoring, or do you feel that you have the right to pick whatever you want to watch at the end of a long workday? Do you watch things on TV that you wouldn't want your children to watch with you? Do you fill your mind with programs that feature unrealistic, immoral relationships among the characters, while nourishing a materialistic outlook by means of the car commercials between scenes?

Television is no respecter of persons. Its ability to consume and destroy is not limited to just the children. Men and women are being snared daily by the traps of TV. Since you are the one designated to hold the spiritual umbrella of protection over your family, if you fail to do so, your family is going to be exposed to some very harmful things.

Your Talk Talks, and Your Walk Talks

If the husband, the leader of the home, has appalling or questionable TV viewing habits, he makes the wife's job of screening the children's programs that much harder. The lack of a good example in this area can also discourage the wife from making wise viewing choices as well.

Leadership in any situation always has a trickle-down effect. As the leader goes, so go the followers. If you, husband, have low TV viewing standards, don't count on your family to have higher standards and don't be surprised by the foul atmosphere created by such a lack.

The producers and directors of today's television shows have "conceived mischief, and brought forth falsehood" (Ps. 7:14). Since the lifestyles of the people at the top are often filled with self-serving iniquity, the fruit of their hands matches the condition of their hearts—barren and empty.

Your family is unimportant to the average TV executive. Your money, on the other hand, is of great value to those in the television industry, and they will use any means necessary to get you to part with it. If it costs you a stable family—oh, well, too bad! After all, one of the first things the television moguls do when accused of contributing to the crudeness of the lives of Americans is to hide behind their standard statement: "You don't *have* to watch TV."

Every man who is a husband or father will have to decide for himself and for his family what the law of the home is going to be regarding TV. Set your standards high, discuss them in detail with your wife (remembering that she will often be left alone to enforce them), and then make a commitment to 'set no wicked thing before your eyes.' Your family needs *you* to carry the banner. It is not the job of your wife, the helpmeet, to set these standards; but she can help you to maintain them, once they are established.

I am certain that I am not advising you leaders on anything

that you don't already know. I am therefore pleading with you *to act on what you know.*

"Ye therefore, beloved, seeing ye know these things before, beware lest ye also, being led away with the error of the wicked, fall from your own stedfastness" (II Pet. 3:17).

Too many families are 'falling from their own steadfastness' today, and much of the blame can be placed squarely on the low standards being maintained in the home. You can take your family to church, but if you saturate them with worldly philosophies and lifestyles via the TV, the church will have much less influence on them.

"Choose You This Day Whom Ye Will Serve"

The television has no power when it is turned off or unplugged. You can determine how much power it will have in your home, and when. You can either invite the enemy in electronically, or you can shut him out. The choice is yours, but doing nothing is not an option. You will not be able to live yesterday again. If you are slothful in establishing wholesome TV standards now, you will wake up one day, and your young people will be too old to listen and too stubborn to heed. You will have produced your very own pack of rebels, with a frustrated, embittered wife thrown in at no extra charge.

Home can be a wonderful refuge. It can be a place of refreshing for those in the ministry who pass through our towns, as well as a center for various church activities such as family potlucks and youth group singspirations. A home that is pure and holy is fit for such use, but a home that is perverted by TV filth emits that uncleanness even if you try to cover it up by turning the TV off when guests are present.

You simply *cannot* hide impurity very convincingly. If nothing else, the lack of Holy Spirit presence in your home will tell on you.

A Christian wife will go where a Christian husband leads. A part of this leadership includes setting the guidelines for the use of various media items in the home. From the TV to the computer, these items are potentially hazardous and require clear usage regulations.

Have you thought about this area of your home yet? Perhaps after reading this brief note of appeal, you will prayerfully consider a plan and will share it with your wife. Then, as a team that God calls "one flesh," you can work together at establishing new standards of purity in your home.

Christian songwriter Philip P. Bliss wrote "Hold the Fort." The second verse sounds a lot like where our homes are today:

See the mighty host advancing,
Satan leading on;
Mighty men around us falling,
Courage almost gone!

Mr. Bliss described a scene of near destruction and despair; but then, thanks be to God, he followed with this chorus:

"Hold the fort, for I am coming,"
Jesus signals still;
Wave the answer back to Heaven,
"By Thy grace, we will."

Are you holding the fort, or are you surrendering it to the enemy? Are you protecting and guarding your families, or are you leaving them open to attack and expecting them to survive the battle without you? Do you truly believe in your heart that Jesus means it when He says that He is coming again? If so, in what shape will He find you and your family when He returns?

Your marriage and family are worth the effort that it will take to bring the electronic appliance called television under your command. Consider this well, make a decision and map your strategy while you still have time.

You have a choice: Either control the remote, or live under remote control.

"Beloved, follow not that which is evil, but that which is good. He that doeth good is of God: but he that doeth evil hath not seen God."—III John 11.

For a complete list of books available from the Sword of the Lord, write to Sword of the Lord Publishers, P. O. Box 1099, Murfreesboro, Tennessee 37133.

(800) 251-4100
(615) 893-6700
FAX (615) 848-6943
www.swordofthelord.com